A GRIM ALMANAC OF

GLASGOW

A GRIM ALMANAC OF

GLASGOW

LYNNE WILSON

The
History
Press

First published 2012

The History Press
The Mill, Brimscombe Port
Stroud, Gloucestershire, GL5 2QG
www.thehistorypress.co.uk

British Library Cataloguing in Publication Data.
A catalogue record for this book is available from the British Library.

ISBN 978 0 7524 6194 6

Typesetting and origination by The History Press
Printed in Great Britain

CONTENTS

ACKNOWLEDGEMENTS

I would like to thank the following organisations for their assistance:

The National Library of Scotland
The British Library
The Scotsman
Glasgow Herald
The National Archives of Scotland
The Scottish Prison Service

With additional thanks to: The British Library for the use of the *Illustrated Police News* images, Transport Scotland for the use of the Dixon's No. 5 Coal Pit image, Ben Brooksbank for the use of the image looking westwards down the Broomielaw and to Dave Hitchbourne for the use of the image of a Victorian prison cell.

All other images used in this book are either copyright free or are from the author's own collection.

INTRODUCTION

The City of Glasgow, known as the 'Second City of the Empire' for much of the Victorian era, grew as a centre of Scotland's transatlantic trade with the Industrial Revolution making the city well known for its shipbuilding and heavy industry. At this time, Glasgow was described as 'one of the finest and richest cities in Europe' and was thought to be a great example of an industrial society. Additionally, the city flourished with great museums, galleries, parks and libraries.

Today, Glasgow remains a vibrant, cosmopolitan city filled with culture and visited by people from all over the world. However, things were not always this way, as Glasgow, like most other cities, had its dark and difficult beginnings. In the 1820s and 1830s, a rapid increase in population created social difficulties with housing conditions becoming cramped and epidemics of cholera and typhus rife among the Glasgow people. From the squalid lodging houses shared by several families, hotbeds of poverty, crime and destitution grew. The Industrial Revolution of the nineteenth century brought more mechanisation to the workplace, replacing many workers with machines, and adding to the existing problem of unemployment. This was highlighted in an article in the *Glasgow Herald* at the time:

> Work cannot be found for many thousands who have been tempted to leave the rural districts, and as a consequence there is misery, crime, disease and poverty in its most helpless form. The first great cause is the miserably low rate of wages paid in the rural districts, where men are quite unable to buy more than the barest necessities of life for their families. The poor hear that better money may be earned in towns, and without knowing anything of the increased expense of living in large cities – an expense which often more than outweighs any increase of wages – they flock in to swell the already over-charged congregation of labour. The railways are greatly responsible for this, as they have done more than anything else to drain the rural districts to keep up their supplies of guards, signalmen and porters. It is not however, in this respect that the mischief is done as in the congregating together of herds of

Kelvingrove Museum, Glasgow.

unskilled men who can do nothing more that dig with a spade of carry bricks up a ladder. So much is now done by machinery that was formerly done by hand that there is not sufficient work to employ the excessive crowd. As a consequence, they starve. Their homes have been broken up and they cannot return to the country, and they remain a disgrace and a danger to the city they have chosen as their habitation.

These conditions were not alleviated quickly, and as the population of Glasgow grew to over one million during the Victorian era, crime, suicide and poverty existed alongside the booming industrial wealth and reputation of the city. At this time, many Irish immigrants settled in Glasgow to find work in the growing industries. With immigrants from both Southern Ireland and Ulster, there were inevitably clashes between people of Catholic and Protestant faiths, often involving men from different factions getting into fights, particularly when they were under the influence of alcohol.

The link between alcohol abuse and crime in general was a subject often debated in the newspapers throughout this time, with the following letter to the editor of the *Caledonian Mercury* newspaper appearing in 1845, from a Glasgow resident, on the subject of those sent to prison for crimes relating to drunkenness:

Very many of those persons committed for drunkenness are heads of families, and not a few of them very young – sometimes mere children; and any one at all capable of reflecting, may easily conceive that a fearful amount of sin, of moral degradation, and of physical suffering and ruin of all kinds, must be the result of such habits. Many a distressing scene takes place here by ragged, miserable, starving and worse that orphan children, coming to ask after and clamour for their drunken and depraved parents, and by many a weeping and heart broken wife following her wretched partner to the gates. I fear that nothing like an extensive and moral renovation of society can be reasonably expected whilst the facilities for intemperance are so great.

Some social improvements were starting to show in the late nineteenth century and, with the demand for labour outstripping supply and many workers were able to negotiate better working conditions. The first medical officer of health was also appointed in 1862 and a slum clearance began under the City Improvement Act of 1866. Other benefits to the city were also in place by the start of the twentieth century with the introduction of a gas supply, electricity and tramways.

Advances were also evident in the way crime was dealt with in Glasgow, with the Glasgow Police Act coming into force in 1800. For most of the Georgian period, watchmen had been used to guard the streets at night, but the new act established the 'City of Glasgow Police', described as the first municipal police force, with the first 'criminal officer' or detective, being appointed in 1819. The Glasgow Police originally looked after the city centre only until 1846 when they merged with the Gorbals, Calton and Anderston Burgh Police. Continual expansion of the city boundaries meant that more and more areas were coming under the control of the Glasgow Police, culminating in a merger with Govan and Partick Burgh Police in 1919.

The remit of the early police also extended to maintaining sanitary conditions, and police duties included: 'Watching, Lighting, Cleansing, Regulation of the Keeping of Pigs, Asses, Dogs, and other inferior animals; Regulation of the lodging houses for the poorer classes; and preventing the undue accumulation of filth or manure'. The job of police constable was not a well-paid position, and, with the long working hours, the police force in the early part of Victoria's reign often consisted of recruits who were less than suitable; and it was not uncommon to see constables appearing in court for crimes they themselves had committed.

Sauchihall Street.

Municipal Buildings, George Square.

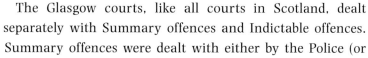

The Glasgow courts, like all courts in Scotland, dealt separately with Summary offences and Indictable offences. Summary offences were dealt with either by the Police (or Burgh) Court or the Sheriff Court. These ranged from the more petty offences to assaults. Indictable offences were dealt with by the Sheriff and Jury Court or the Circuit Court of Justiciary. As the only High Court of Justiciary for Scotland was in Edinburgh, the Circuit Court would come to other cities routinely to hear the more serious cases, typically serious assaults, fraud or murder, until such time as Glasgow had its own permanent High Court. It was not unusual at this time to receive a fairly lengthy prison sentence for crimes which we would probably describe as 'petty' today; however, it was also common for fairly serious assaults to receive a comparatively lenient sentence, with crimes of theft being seen, particularly in the Victorian period, as one of the worst offences against a person.

Many people ended up in the justice system – from those who stole food in a desperate attempt to feed their families and keep them out of the workhouse, to violent people often under the influence of alcohol, assaulting their spouses or associates. A lack of proper treatment and understanding of mental illness, would also result in some unfortunate characters ending up in the justice system.

For 'capital' crimes such as murder and rape during the Georgian and Victorian periods, the sentence which normally resulted was that of death. Almost every society has used the sentence of capital punishment at one time and in Britain it became a cause for concern that juries may be acquitting criminals, rather than convict them knowing they would face execution. Public hangings, which had been the norm in Glasgow, were eventually replaced by executions inside the prisons in 1868. These public executions tended to draw large crowds of spectators, and were seen by some as entertainment. There were many who were critical of these public executions. On 9 May 1838, an article appeared in the *Edinburgh Evening*

Courant, on 'The Punishment of Death', which described the practice as a 'hideous spectacle' designed to let the public 'feed upon the agony of the wretch', and also highlighted that murders were less frequent in the countries where the punishment of death did not exist. It was also noticed that violent crime seemed to increase around the time of executions. With public hangings, scaffolds with platforms were erected in towns, to which the criminal would be brought to face their punishment. The criminal would have a hood placed over their head and the noose would be placed around the neck. The prisoner would then indicate that they were ready by dropping a handkerchief. With the long drop hanging, the neck would be dislocated and the spinal cord snapped, causing an instant death if done properly. This was thought to be a more humane method than the shorter drop, in which death was caused by suffocation from the noose round the neck. When hangings began taking place

Left: A nineteenth-century hanging.

Below: Hungry children – desperate times called for desperate thefts. (From *London Illustrated News*)

The Tolbooth Steeple, all that remains today
of the Tolbooth Prison.

within the prisons instead, a black flag was raised to let the public know
that the execution had been carried out.

At one time in Glasgow there were eight prisons, with the oldest being the
Tolbooth, at Glasgow Cross, the steeple of which remains today. All of these
prisons had closed by 1840 except the North Prison or Bridewell at Duke
Street and the Burgh Prison at Glasgow Green. Due to overcrowding in these
two Glasgow prisons, Barlinnie Prison was built in 1880, which is still in
place today.

One of the main concerns with prisons in the nineteenth century was the
association of criminals, and it was decided that the less association they had
together, the less chance there was of prisons becoming a training ground
in all aspects of criminality. There were also growing concerns during this
time as to the number of children serving prison sentences. Captain Kincaid,
an Inspector of Prisons, highlighted this in 1849 in his report on Scottish
Prisons, in which he spoke of the 'defective state of the laws of Scotland in
their provisions for the punishment of juvenile offences'. Captain Kincaid

A drawing depicting child labour from 1913.

expressed concern over several cases he had become aware of where children had been committed to prison for very trivial acts, such as one child who served fourteen days for stealing apples. It was recognised at the time that juvenile offenders were often neglected children with no one to protect or care for them, and Kincaid thought that a better system would be to place these children in a reformatory school. This, he believed, would educate them and provide them with trades, skills and discipline so that they might go on to lead a more productive life. The cost of providing these schools was more cost effective in the long run if the children could be reformed, instead of becoming habitual criminals and having to be maintained by the public for life. Kincaid also observed that more had to be done in communities, to make 'worthless parents do their duty'. This idea of reformatory schools was a popular one and in 1850, following the report of a Parliamentary Committee on Criminal and Destitute Children, a bill was introduced 'for the better care and reformation of juvenile offenders', by establishing reformatory schools for young people, under sixteen years of age, convicted of offences under Summary Procedure.

The connection between poverty and crime, and debate on the ways to break this cycle, have been explored throughout the ages and appeared as the subject of an article in a newspaper in 1874:

> Workhouses, gaols and penitentiaries are somehow, in this age of advanced civilisation, prominent and most unpleasant 'institutions'... Charity and compassion are all very well in their place; but you may so overdose a people with institutions for their assistance, as to entirely take out of them the spirit of self reliance and energy; and you may go on to such a pitch with reformation schemes as to induce the belief in the lower classes that everything for their welfare depends upon other people, that no responsibility whatever rests upon themselves, and that whilst even being improved they ought to be supported at the expense of society.

However, crime, poverty and suicides were not the only grim aspects of Glasgow's past. Like any emerging city, Glasgow had its share of accidents, particularly industrial accidents. For most of the working classes, work was a significant hazard, and long hours, tiredness and a lack of any regard to safety by often unscrupulous employers resulted in horrific accidents in the workplace. Children in particular were at risk, as due to their small size they were used, particularly in the Victorian era, to clean inside machinery, often with disastrous consequences. Child labour in general was a practice many social reformers of the time wanted to see end, such as the writer of the following letter to the editor of the *Glasgow Herald* in 1872, speaking out against objections to the Factory Act which aimed to prevent a child under thirteen years of age from working more that six and a half hours a day. The particular example this local resident gives is of children working in printworks:

> To take a child of eight years out of its warm bed at six o'clock in the morning and make it hang over a colour tub till six o'clock in the evening and they say "it is not unhealthy work", is to say the least of it, sad ignorance. No one will welcome the new Act more joyfully than the poor children; and God knows it is them who need their hours of labour shortened instead of their (too often)

lazy fathers. Many at their early age sow the seeds of disease they never throw off, and drop into an early grave. I know what it is, and to this day feel its consequences.

In this book, grim events from the Georgian era right through to the Edwardian era give us an insight into the darker side of the past of this great city. From murder most foul to terrible accidents along with tales of execution, poverty, crime and other macabre events, this book contains all things 'grim' about Glasgow's past.

Lynne Wilson, 2012

JANUARY

Sauchiehall Street in winter.

1 JANUARY

1861 The trial of a young man named John McFadyen was heard. McFadyen, who was described as having 'a dull, stupid-looking expression', was accused of having stripped a two-and-a-half-year-old boy named Alexander Shields of his clothes, thrown him into the deep water of the River Clyde and held him under the water with a long stick until he died. From the evidence given, it appeared that the child had left his parents' house for the purpose of meeting his father on his way home for dinner. When he did not return, a search was made and the grim events uncovered. McFadyen had met the child in Commercial Road, Hutchesontown, lifted him in his arms and carried him to the river side, opposite Clydevale Works. There, he stripped off the boy's clothes, threw him into the water and held him underneath with a stick. A young man who was on the opposite side of the river, saw McFadyen with the stick, but had thought that he was about to commence fishing. Once he had finished drowning the child, McFadyen ran up the embankment and told two girls he met that a woman had drowned a child, and if they came to the river side he would point out the place. Once they were distracted with this, he grabbed the boy's clothes and ran off with them. He had not proceeded very far, however, when he was met by the boy's mother, who upon seeing her son's clothes in McFadyen's possession, asked him what had happened to her child. McFadyen told her the same story he had told the girls; however, by this time the young man from across the river had arrived on the scene and realising something was wrong, confronted him. McFadyen eventually confessed to what he had done, although he could give no explanation for why he had carried out this murderous act. During the trial several surgeons gave the opinion that although he was 'of a weak mind', McFadyen was not insane. The jury returned a verdict of guilty and the judge promptly sentenced the unemotional McFadyen to death.

Newspaper heading
of the crime.

HORRIBLE MURDER AND MUTILATION IN GLASGOW.
A WOMAN SAWN TO PIECES.

2 JANUARY

1893 William McKeown, a gardner, and Thomas McNeilly, a sailor, were tried at the Glasgow Judiciary Court on a charge of murdering Eliza O'Connor 'under horrible circumstances'. The body of the victim had been mutilated in an apartment within West Lodge Villa, Pollockshields, and buried in four different holes in the garden behind the house.

McKeown, in whose room the murder was committed, had attempted to flee to Paisley the following day, but had been captured, and on his capture, he had tried to commit suicide by cutting his throat. In the course of the police enquiries, it had been ascertained that McNeilly, a friend of McKeown's, had also been present. McKeown, who had a white bandage round this head to support the wound on his throat, pleaded not guilty to manslaughter; however, this plea was not accepted and the case went to trial. Much evidence was given by witnesses which placed McKeown at the scene of the crime and evidence was given by Dr Samuel Johnston Moore, the medical examiner for the Crown, that the body of the deceased had been cut up and that death had occurred due to the severing of the carotid arteries of the neck. McNeilly was dismissed from the proceedings by Lord Adam, who stated that the court had heard nothing to incriminate him in the matter, and the case against McKeown continued. His defence was that he and Eliza, with whom he was in a relationship, had been quarrelling and he had struck her, but had not intended to kill her. The jury after an absence of half an hour, found McKeown guilty and he was sentenced to death.

3 JANUARY

1847 A young married woman, residing at 81 Carrick Street, met her death under horrific circumstances. While sitting sewing by the fire, the woman's two-year-old daughter was amusing herself at the fire with a piece of lighted paper and somehow set fire to her mother's gown. In a few minutes she was covered in flames, and in that state ran firstly into a neighbour's house, then into the street, burning from head to foot. A man who was passing at the time, threw her down on the street and extinguished the flames; however, she was so dreadfully burned that she died the same evening.

4 JANUARY

1850   At around seven o'clock in the morning, the inhabitants of Bath Street and the streets in the vicinity were thrown into a state of panic and confusion by a tremendous explosion, followed by a rumbling noise, which sounded like an earthquake. In many of the houses, the glass in every apartment was smashed, and, in some instances, the window frames forced out. The cause of this had been an accidental explosion of gas, which had supposedly been accumulating for the few days prior to the incident, with the smell having become so offensive that it raised the concerns of the residents. On the morning of the incident, three men had entered an underground vault used as an ice store, to collect a supply of ice, and had no sooner entered the vault when the explosion took place. It was thought that this was the origin of the explosion, as a gas pipe in that area had been observed for some time to have become bent due to subsidence. In the course of the afternoon, the scene of the devastation was visited by great numbers of people, who were anxious to view the effects of the explosion.

5 JANUARY

1895   Matthew Jordan, described as 'an old pensioner', was remanded in custody on a charge of having murdered a woman named Mrs Gray and severely injured her husband the previous night. The Grays resided at 8 Bedford Street, on the same floor as Jordan, and after the couple had gone to bed, Jordan began to shout and sing at the top of his voice. Mr Gray went out and asked him to be quiet, but it appeared that Jordan, without making any reply, rushed at Mr Gray and stabbed him repeatedly with a large bread knife. Mr Gray managed to summon a policeman; however, his wife, on coming out to find out what the commotion was, was stabbed by Jordan seven times. Mrs Gray later died in the infirmary. Matthew Jordan was seventy-three years old.

Newspaper headline from around the time of Mrs Gray's murder.

SHOCKING TRAGEDY IN GLASGOW.

6 JANUARY   **1848**   On this night, the wife of Charles Log, a bricklayer, had occasion to go out of her house on an errand, leaving her two children aged eight and six, on their own. Soon after she had left the house, the neighbours were alerted by loud screams and cries of 'fire!' coming from the house. The door was burst open, and it was found that the eldest girl had gone too close to the fire and her clothes had caught alight. The child, in her terror rushed out when the door was opened and ran through the close in flames. Despite medical help arriving promptly, she had received so much injury that she died in the early hours of the next morning.

7 JANUARY   **1850**   A woman residing in Bishop Street, Anderston, met her death in what was described as 'a very melancholy manner'. Being slightly the worse of liquor at the time of the accident, whilst endeavouring to swallow a mouthful of black pudding, she choked on the food which had stuck in her throat. The poor woman, despite medical aid having been obtained, died within a few minutes, after 'enduring all the agonies of suffocation'.

8 JANUARY   **1850**   At the Police Court on this date, three miners were fined three guineas each or the alternative of sixty days' imprisonment, for a 'most unprovoked and cruel assault' upon Hugh Montgomery, a carrier between Eaglesham and Glasgow, and Robert Arneil, a mason, in the Gorbals. It appeared that Montgomerty had been returning home via the Gorbals, accompanied by Arneil, when without warning they were set upon, knocked down and savagely beaten by the prisoners, who it was noted 'had not even the excuse of intoxication'.

9 JANUARY   **1849**   An 'Atrocious Case' of 'Drunken Women' appeared in the Police Court on this date. The *Glasgow Herald* newspaper began the report on this story by commenting that 'the most degraded, senseless, shameless, conscienceless specimen of the human family is a drunken woman'. It seems that the two women in question had been selected by the Parochial Inspector to act as nurses in the House of Recovery, preparing for patients suffering from cholera. However, within a short time, these 'nurses' had begun stealing bed clothes, dishes, chairs and other items from the House of Recovery piece by piece in order to pawn them for whisky. This continued until they were detected in the very act. They were sentenced to fifteen days' imprisonment.

10 JANUARY

1853 At the Anderston Police Court, three Irishmen described as 'brawny', were charged with 'a most unprovoked and brutal attack' on a number of trades people the previous Saturday night. From the evidence, it appeared that the injured parties, who had been spending their Saturday evening in the town, were quietly returning homewards by Main Street, Anderston, when one of them overheard a man at the opposite side of the street say to a companion, 'We'll follow, and give them a welting.' A watchman who happened to be near was told of this and on recognising the man pointed out to him as a 'notorious character', he summoned two other constables to assist him. This was fortunate timing as a few moments later the screams of the females in the party were heard. The night was almost pitch dark, but the constables running up soon put a stop the violence, and with the assistance of the workmen, took the men into custody. The workmen could not understand the reason for the attack, as not a word had been interchanged between the two parties. The men, who were no strangers to the courtroom, were sentenced to sixty days' imprisonment. One of them, it was reported, had previously been convicted nine times for similar offences.

11 JANUARY

1932 After a trial lasting five days, thirty-one-year-old Peter Queen, the son of a turf commission agent, was found guilty by a majority verdict in the Glasgow High Court, of the murder of Christina Gall, aged twenty-seven. Christina Gall, who had been living with Queen in lodgings in Dumbarton Road, was found in a bed strangled, with a piece of cord tied tightly around her neck. The jury took two hours to consider their verdict on this case, which was complicated by the fact that when the woman was found, there was no disturbance of the bed clothing or the clothing she was wearing. Additionally, as no furniture had been disturbed and there were no marks upon her body, the defence argued that no violence had taken place and that Christina Gall had committed suicide. Evidence given by Sir Bernard Spilsbury, a leading name in the emerging forensic science at the time, also pointed to suicide. Despite this, however, Queen was found guilty and, as was usual for the time, sentenced to death.

12 JANUARY **1849**   A case of the Victorian crime of 'child stripping' occurred on this date. While a little boy was proceeding along Rutherglen Loan with some groceries and a small sum of money, he was approached by a young female, who, under the pretence that she had something to give him, lured the child into a common stair in the neighbourhood. Once there, she stole the groceries and money from him, then ran off with his clothing.

13 JANUARY **1850**   The lower part of the High Street, particularly in the neighbourhood of Close No. 90, was noted at this time to have become so notorious for thefts, assaults and robberies, that neither male nor female, young or old, were safe in passing it at night. On this date, while a gentleman was passing along High Street, around five o'clock in the afternoon, he was assaulted by two females, who were soon joined by one of the young thieves known for prowling that area. The trio knocked him down, kicked and beat him, with one of the assailants biting the man's thumb into the bone. They were all sentenced to sixty days' imprisonment.

14 JANUARY **1856**   Whilst James Dugall, a hand on board a dredging machine in the Steamboat Wharf, North Quay, was hauling in one of the mooring lines, he raised the body of a man to the surface of the water. A small boat was obtained and the body was brought on board. On being taken to the Clyde Police Office, the man was identified as forty-six-year-old James Lee, a carter, who had gone missing on the evening of New Year's Day.

15 JANUARY **1849**   James McKissock, of the firm of James McKissock & Co., manufacturers, found himself in the Police Office, charged with assaulting Sheriff Officer Thomas White. McKissock had previously been brought before the sheriff for examination, but declined answering the questions set to him, and was therefore sent to prison. After a day or two in prison, McKissock had expressed his readiness to answer the questions as required and he was collected from the prison by the Sheriff Officer. On the way to court, McKissock was permitted to call at his house in London Street, for the purpose of changing his clothes. While doing so however, he demanded to see the warrant, which on it being produced by the officer, he took hold of it and promptly tore it into pieces, despite the officer trying to secure it. A struggle then ensued in which the officer was severely assaulted. McKissock was sent back to prison to await trial at a higher court.

16 JANUARY

Glasgow Institutions - Duke Street Prison

The Duke Street Prison was one of eight prisons which previously served the city of Glasgow and the surrounding area. Also known as the Bridewell or Northern Prison, the institution was known for its terrible living conditions, and, although improvements were made to the structure of the building over the years, the conditions inside it did not improve. By 1840, Duke Street was one of only two prisons in Glasgow, the other being Glasgow Green Prison, also known as the Burgh Prison or Southern Prison, which closed in 1863. Following a transfer of responsibility to the state from the local authorities, another prison, HM Prison Barlinnie, was built in 1882 in the east of the city. Most of the prisoners from Duke Street Prison transferred to this new jail, with the exception of the women, as the Bridewell remained open as a women's prison until 1955.

Some of the women held at Duke Street were political activists and suffragettes, who instigated the closure of the prison after continual protests against the living conditions. As a result, the site was finally demolished in 1958.

Despite the conditions, Glasgow Bridewell was known as one of the most ordered prisons of the time. It was also one of the first to have the 'separate system', which was introduced in 1825 by William Brebner, the governor at the time. The separate system took the form of prisoners having a cell to themselves, with no association with one another during their sentence in order that they spent the time reflecting on their wrongdoings, with even daily exercise being taken in silence. This system was criticised by some as cruel, and the isolation was thought to lead prisoners to insanity. Frederick Hill, the Inspector of Prisons, was very much in favour of this system for all prisons in Scotland, however, and later stated that the isolation:

> ... should always be accompanied with useful employment, instruction, opportunities of reading, frequent visits of officers,

and daily exercise in the open air. Not however, that I think we should always wait until all these accessories can be obtained; for so great are the evils of association among criminals, that it in my opinion it is better to dispense with one or two of these than to allow such evils to continue.

The 'useful employment' usually consisted of stone breaking, net making or picking oakum, all of which were thought to 'improve the health of prisoners, make them sleep soundly, and to prevent a nervous and restless condition, adverse to good discipline and moral reformation'. The separate system was in place for much of the nineteenth century, although it often proved difficult to enforce due to the number of prisoners greatly exceeding the number of cells in prisons such as the Bridewell.

17 JANUARY

1839 A melancholy case of the murder of a deaf and dumb girl by her own brother was reported on this date. Thomas McKinnis, a shoemaker residing in King Street, called at the house of an acquaintance in the Saltmarket and informed him that his sister was dead. When this acquaintance asked how this had happened, McKinnis replied that he had 'caused her death by his own hands'. The acquaintance communicated this information to McKinnis' brother, a 'respectable person in town' and the police were informed. Thomas McKinnis and his sister had resided alone in the same house and according to his statement, he loved his sister and only committed the act 'for her good', as he had tried unsuccessfully to get her admitted to the deaf and dumb institution, and was afraid that 'she might come to want'. On arriving at the house in King Street, the superintendent found the grisly scene, with the naked body of Helen McKinnis on the floor, drenched in blood and covered with wounds. She had received three wounds in the abdomen and several other cuts about the neck. Neighbours had heard Helen crying out sometime between 1 and 2 o'clock in the morning, but as the cries almost immediately ceased they thought nothing of it. It was reported that McKinnis had recently been troubled with 'religious melancholy' and had often behaved disorderly in the house, with a previous episode involving him attempting to set fire to his furniture.

18 JANUARY

1847 A report of two attempted street robberies was given on this date in the *Glasgow Herald*. The first case occurred about seven o'clock on the previous Sunday evening, whilst a gentleman was returning from Govan. He was attacked by a person described as a 'ruffianly fellow', about six feet tall, who seized him, and ordered him to 'deliver up', meaning hand over his valuables. A struggle ensued, in which the attacker struck the gentleman a blow which stunned him, and proceeded to rifle his pockets. However, frustrated that the man's coat was buttoned, and, on hearing others coming to assist, the assailant ran off. It was reported that a retuned convict answering to his description had been lurking about in the area. The second attempted robbery occurred on the previous Thursday at around five o'clock in the afternoon, when a gentleman residing in Cleland Street, Hutchesontown, was attacked by two 'ruffians' on entering the passage leading to his own house. While one held his arms, the other seized his watch guard, which fortunately snapped, saving his watch. Concern was rising at this time due to the number crimes of this nature taking place, with the Citizen commenting that 'when such outrages are perpetrated, not in a corner, but at a man's own door, and almost in open day, who is safe from attack?'

19 JANUARY   1826   At Belvidere Colliery, to the east of the city, an alarming incident occurred. The colliery, which had not been working for three weeks previous, had undergone repair, and during that time the hard coal, 30 inches thick, filled with water. When the water was drawn away, the roof of the pit had become soft and stones had fallen from it, obstructing the proper current of free air. On this morning, some of the colliers descended the pit for the purposes of opening the trap doors to clear the air course, and remove the stones that had fallen from the roof. The workmen had proceeded from the pit bottom, on their way to the work rooms, about 60 or 70 yards, when they encountered fire damp. Several of them inhaled the 'impure air' and on returning to the bottom of the pit, it was found that three of them were missing. One of the men was found and given life-saving treatment, but on attempting to recover the two others, three more men were overpowered. News of this incident had reached the family and friends of those working in the pit, who started arriving from all quarters.

By the exertions of the other workmen from the pit and some volunteers, four of the five men missing were brought up in an exhausted state, and all recovered. The men who had volunteered to find them were repeatedly overcome by the 'foul air', but had repeatedly come back up, recovered and went back down until the missing men had been found. The only remaining collier in the pit, a young man by the name of Sharp, could not be found that night. He was one of those who had gone down to save the missing men, and to the astonishment of everyone present, he was discovered breathing after being trapped for twenty-six hours in the pit.

20 JANUARY

1826 During the night a man and a woman, who had undertaken to watch a corpse in a house in Saltmarket Street, exhausted with fatigue from having performed this function for two nights previous, both fell fast asleep. When they awoke, they found 'to their utter astonishment' that some thieves had been in the house, and had stolen the sheet that covered the corpse, two bottles of whisky, a dram glass and a pair of brass candlesticks.

21 JANUARY

1854 A little boy named Sweenie, described as 'poorly clad, but of smart intelligent appearance' was brought before the Police Court on a charge of stealing a cotton gown from a woman named Shaw, a pastry baker in Saltmarket Street. The boy denied the theft, but the charge was proven. His mother, described as 'a poor, thin, sickly looking woman, sharp featured and very intelligent' came forward at this stage and addressed the court, explaining:

> I am a widow woman. My husband died about two years since, and I reside in Saltmarket Street. I have not a house of my own, but lodge in a room there. This boy is 12 years of age and was working along with his brother (who is two years younger) in Bell's Pottery. It appears they have done no work since New Year's Day, although they have come home regularly to their meals as if they had been working. They earn each 3s a week, and on Saturday last I only found out they had not been at work, when I went expecting to get 10s, but found they had earned nothing. This boy has led off his brother. I have a young

child at home just now in a dying state, and I fear I have been too long away from it.

22 JANUARY   **1847** On this morning, it was discovered that a horse and Harrington vehicle had by some means been immersed in the basin of the Paisley and Johnstone Canal, at Port Eglinton. The horse was found to have drowned, and on subsequent search, the dead body of the driver was found near the same spot. The driver, forty-year-old Andrew Douglas, had been employed by Walker of the Bazaar, in Nile Street. He had gone out to the west end of Sauchiehall Road with a company, whom he set down at their residence around half past twelve in the morning. From there, Sauchiehall Street would have been his nearest road to return to the stables; however, it was under repair at the time, therefore Douglas had taken the route by North Street. With Douglas falling asleep due to the late hour, the horse continued to go on until it turned into Port Eglinton, and walked in the dark into the canal. A woman had observed what was about to happen, but was unable to give warning in time.

23 JANUARY   **1855** Janet Love, described as being 'much addicted to intemperance', was burned to death in her own dwelling house, whilst drunk. Mrs Love was found by her husband when he returned home from work, her ears and nose having been burned off. It was supposed that her clothes must have caught fire.

24 JANUARY   **1912** In the Hilhead district of Glasgow, a middle-aged man named George Riddoch, a printer and engraver, was murdered while walking through a narrow lane leading to the university. Mr Riddoch was unmarried and had resided at the Young Men's Christian Association Club for several years. He was keenly interested in the Scottish Aeronautical Society, and was the chairman of the Model Aero Club. At the time he met his death, he was returning from the society's workshops. A young woman heard a scuffle from her bedroom, and after raising the window, shouted that she would call the police. Just then, the assailant raised his hand and struck Mr Riddoch on the head with a heavy instrument, the blow exposing his brain. The attacker ran off in the direction of the university and escaped.

25 JANUARY   **1797** James McKaen was executed at the Cross of Glasgow on this date for the murder and robbery of James Buchanan. McKaen's

Glasgow University.

body was given to the Professor of Anatomy for dissection, which was usual at this time, due to the limited availability of corpses for medical study. McKaen's confession was featured in the press:

> I James McKaen, aged 44 years, was Born in Glasgow, of reputable parents, my father died when I was three years old and soon after my mother made a second marriage with a Book-printer in Glasgow, my stepfather lived but short time, and I got my education in the time of her second widowhood, which was common reading and writing. My mother made a third marriage with a journeyman shoemaker, whom she set up as a master in Paisley. He behaved extremely ill to her [...] and then ran off and was never more heard of.

When I was ten years old, I was bound an apprentice for seven years, to Mr. William Greenlees shoemaker in Glasgow, but he failing in trade my indenture was destroyed, when I had served only two years of the time; I was then sent by my friends to Dalkeith, where my mother bound me an apprentice to Mr. John Cowan, for two years more, which time I served out all but three weeks, when I went to Lanark, I got work there from a very good master for two years, and then returned to my mother at Dalkeith. She gave me too much liberty with pocket-money which made me fall into loose company. When I was sixteen years old, I courted a sober young girl at Dalkeith, but having no real love to her in my heart. [...] At one period of my life, being at Musselburgh with an acquaintance who was enlisting with a party of Frazer's Highlanders [...] an attempt was made to enlist or entangle a friend of mine and me who had come together with the Recruit, and the landlord of the house where the party were drinking, wishing to second their design of entangling us, came in and declared 'we were all the king's men together.' I was so provoked at this conduct of the landlord, that I threw the candlestick at him with such violence, that it cut him thro' the check bone...

Short time after my marriage with my present wife at Dalkeith, I acknowledge that I termed a criminal correspondence with a young girl in the parish of Libberton which is three miles from Dalkeith, and she bore a child to me, it was a girl, and I, to get rid of the scandal of a child in adultery, made public satisfaction in the parish church of Libberton. I know that I have been accused of the murder of his child; But I declare, the charge is groundless .[...] With regard to another very heavy charge brought against me by common report, that I drowned my Mother in the great Canal I am free to declare as a dying man, that though I was the person who called her out, I am totally innocent. I acknowledge that the atrocious Murder for which I justly suffer, gives great ground to excite this rumour against me. [...] With regard to the atrocious deed for which I suffer, the Murder of James Buchanan, I confess [...]; yet I deny that I intended or premeditated to take away his life. [...] The reason of my preparing the razor in the manner that I had an altercation with Buchanan on an old grudge 'twixt him and I; the dreadful murder I committed on him. [...] But these various particulars are far too extensive to be set down in the small compass of this speech. I am conscious [...] that there are a variety of reports propagated against me: Such as that I had designed the death of Mr. Alexander, a worthy Surgeon is this city, now deceased. That I had broiled my mother's favourite cat in a pot, and committed many other acts of cruelty. [...] And I declare as a dying man, that every report which may be circulated against me, which is not included in the said narrative, is totally and completely groundless.

With regard to my trial, I confessed my crimes to the court, of course the trial was but short; I experienced every indulgence from the court, my Jury, and the Judges, and I approved of their judgment, for I thanked them in the Court for their decision, after my sentence was repeated. On the 26th of December 1796 I was transmitted back to Glasgow according to my sentence, and was lodged again in the Tolbooth there, where I have at all times received every indulgence that possibly could be given, from the honourable Magistrates, and the Keepers of their Tolbooth. [...] I desire to commit my departing Spirit to God who gave it.

26 JANUARY

1858 A fatal accident occurred in the afternoon, while John Rodger, a gamekeeper was proceeding along Strathaven Road with a loaded gun. It appeared that Rodger had been carrying the gun in a concealed manner, the stock being in one pocket, and the barrel in another. However, he accidentally stumbled and by some means the gun fired, rupturing his bowels and killing him instantly.

27 JANUARY

Glasgow Institutions – The Magdalene Asylum
Established in 1812, the Glasgow Magdalene Asylum opened in response to increasing worries regarding prostitution and the city's resulting 'moral health'. It was thought that the best way to deal with this social problem was to house the 'fallen' women in these voluntary institutions in order to 'save' them from their immoral lives, and try to reform them. Although prostitutes were the main concern, other women such as single mothers and those who were thought to dress immorally were also reformed in the institution. In 1859 the Magdalene Asylum became the Magdalene Institution, and had specific criteria for admittance.

Prospective inmates had to be newly fallen women who were free from syphilis, pregnancy and who were willing to receive the disciplined regime. Through training, the women learned how to 'support themselves honestly', usually being trained to carrying out laundry work, and there was a strong emphasis on religion. The annual report of the Magdalene Institution in 1865, commented on the supposed relationship between alcohol and women's immorality, 'Our uniform experience amounts to this – that if a woman is intercepted at the threshold of the path to drunkenness, however depraved or otherwise vicious she may be, there is hope of reclamation; but if this vice has been confirmed into a habit, recovery is all but hopeless'. An advertisement in 1888 spoke of the institutions successes, stating:

> ... nearly 5,000 young women have shared more or less in the benefits of the Institution since 1859. During the same period, no fewer than 1,080 young women have been restored to parents or friends, and 942 have been placed in domestic service or other respectable employment, while thirty-two were sent abroad, thus making 2,054 who have been rescued from a life of shame and restored to society, after having received the usual education and training in the home.

28 JANUARY   **1853**   In these days of corporal punishment of juvenile offenders, a young thief was sentenced to undergo thirty stripes for picking pockets. As the same boy had received the same punishment only two days previously, The *Guardian* newspaper commented that this punishment was given with too much 'compassionate gentleness' by using an instrument resembling a 'toy lash', and suggested that the authorities use a much harsher instrument instead.

29 JANUARY   **1853**   Another case of 'child stripping' occurred on this date. During the evening, a woman became aware of screams coming from a stair in Gallowgate Street. The screams, which she could tell were that of a little boy, were becoming increasingly more distressed. The woman discovered that the boy had just been stripped of his jacket by a woman named Mary Stewart, who coolly stated that she wanted the garment to put on her own child. Stewart, described by the court as 'heartless', was sentenced to sixty days' imprisonment.

30 JANUARY   1853   A man named John McFarlane, who had been 'rather the worse for his native whisky', walked to the end of the quay into the water. A labourer named Hugh Ferguson and another man, hearing McFarlane's cries for help, instantly jumped in after him and with some difficulty succeeded in bringing him to the shore, where he was taken to the Police Office. Bank receipts to the value of £160, several £1 notes and some silver were found on the obviously wealthy McFarlane. When sober he was asked if he would give the men who rescued him a monetary token of appreciation, as they were poor men and times were very hard. McFarlane scratched his head and gave some thought as to how much he could spare, coming up with the figure of a shilling. After some discussion, however, he was persuaded to value his life at a higher figure, allowing the men two shillings each.

31 JANUARY   1848   On the evening of Hogmanay, a young woman by the name of Rodgers, was sent out by her mother to provide some refreshment for a party that evening. She set of on this errand, taking the quickest route which was along the canal. The young woman, however, never returned. When nothing was heard of her whereabouts during the course of the night, the canal was dragged on New Year's Day and the grim discovery was made.

FEBRUARY

The Marble Staircase, City Chambers.

1 FEBRUARY

1850 For the crimes of forgery and murder, Margaret Hamilton was hanged in front of the courthouse, facing the Green. The circumstances of the crime were that Margaret's sister-in-law, Jean Hamilton, had received the sum of £20, which she lodged in the Strathaven bank, unaware that the deposit receipt had ended up on the possession of Margaret Hamilton. Forging her sister-in-law's name, Margaret drew the money from the bank, then proceeded to poison Jean with arsenic. Margaret Hamilton, having been found guilty, had been sentenced to 'suffer the extreme penalty of the law'. Resigned to the fate awaiting her, Hamilton had been visited by the Revd Mr Gillan of St John's and the Revd Mr Reid, the chaplain of the prisons. Rather than confessing to her crimes however, Hamilton had tried in these conversations to blame one of her husband's relatives for the crime.

In the time leading up to her execution, Hamilton was visited once by the uncle who had brought her up, described as 'a worthy and pious old man', and three times by her husband, Andrew Hamilton. It was reported that on their final meeting, the day prior to the execution, her husband was 'far more affected than she was', pleading with her to admit to the crime she had committed. Still, she refused to do so. On parting from her, Andrew Hamilton 'went into convulsions'; however, Margaret was described as remaining 'as calm as before'.

The gallows were erected in front of the courthouse and at daybreak on the morning of the execution, a considerable number of people began to assemble. Those spectators were described as consisting 'primarily of the lowest classes, with a large sprinkling of old women'. People continued to flock from all quarters of the city, and by eight o'clock there were thought to be around 20,000 spectators present. Meanwhile, Margaret Hamilton who had become faint the previous night at the thought of what was to come, had to be dressed in the morning by prison medical staff, due to her weak disposition. At 7.35 a.m. a service was conducted in the cell by the Revd Mr Gillan. After prayer, Mr Gillan asked if she had anything further to say, to which she faintly whispered, 'No'. Hamilton then partook of a glass of wine and the executioner then arrived in preparation to perform his duty. A little before eight o'clock, the magistates assembled in the courthouse along with representatives from the press. At five minutes past eight, moaning was heard from the narrow underground passage leading from the prison to the courthouse, and the unhappy woman emerged supported by two prison officers, her face pale and

livid. The officers supported her on each side while the executioner put the rope around her neck and pulled the cap over her eyes. Hamilton whispered to the executioner, 'Do it with as little pain as you can.' The officers then left the platform. The chaplain was praying constantly on the step behind her and the executioner offered her the signal handkerchief, which she did not take. As she stood on the drop, she was seen to sway backwards and forwards, finally falling back in a faint and swinging into a recumbent position, supported by the rope, with her feet partially resting on the drop. As gasps of horror were heard across the crowd, the executioner pulled the bolt and the drop fell. Margaret Hamilton died almost instantly. After hanging for forty minutes, the body was taken down and later buried in the prison grounds.

2 FEBRUARY   1922   By this date, the spectacle of the public execution had been banned and criminals sentenced to death were hanged within the

prison walls. William Harkness, condemned to death for murder, was one such person executed in Duke Street Prison in Glasgow. The crime for which he paid 'the last penalty of the law' was the murder of Elizabeth Benjamin, a fourteen-year-old Jewish girl. At the trial, both Harkness and his wife were sentenced to death; however, Mrs Harkness had received a reprieve a few days prior to her execution, and was instead given a period of imprisonment. The motive for their crime had been robbery. A large crowd of people had gathered in Cathedral Square and the vicinity, awaiting the customary raising of the black flag at the prison, signifying the successful delivery of the death sentence. The distance from the cell which housed the condemned man was a walk of only thirty seconds, and Harkness was said to have walked firmly to the scaffold. He had made no confession. Harkness'

CONDEMNED MAN UNMOVED.

Above: A newspaper headline around the time of Harkness' execution.

Below: Cathedral Square today.

death was instantaneous and the black flag was raised at exactly eight o'clock. The crowd, happy that justice had been done, slowly dispersed.

3 FEBRUARY

1826   The body of a man was found on the footpath leading from Hamilton Hill to Keppoch, having the look of a body which had been there for a considerable length of time. From the appearance of the ground around him, it looked as though there had been some sort of violent struggle. His shoes were found nearby, but his hat was nowhere to be seen. From a deep gash in his head, his brain was seen to be protruding. On searching his pockets, nothing was found except for an old key. The body was taken to a nearby public house, where the man was recognised as John Reid, a labourer from Tradeston, Glasgow.

4 FEBRUARY

1850   A boy described as 'respectable', was wandering along the road to Paisley, amusing himself with a pistol. The pistol seems to have gone off by accident, shooting the boy in the left hand and destroying his thumb. Fortunately a lady who was passing at the time, took the little boy on her gig to the residence of Dr McKechnie in Glasgow, where it was found necessary to amputate his thumb. This was carried out under the influence of chloroform, the most common anaesthetic at the time, and, after a short time, the boy was sent on his way home.

5 FEBRUARY

1849   It was discovered in the morning that the premises of Mr Miller, tailor and clothier in Barrhead, had been broken into and a great quantity of merchandise stolen. A person was despatched to the police authorities in Glasgow to give information of the theft. However, on his arrival he found that most of the articles had been recovered and one of the thieves was in custody. At around seven

o'clock that morning Sergeant McColl, while on duty in Crown Street, Hutchesontown, observed a suspicious-looking individual walking briskly along the pavement carrying a well-filled sack on his shoulders. The officer had been following the man a short distance, when the man realised that he was being followed and darted down a lane. This action confirmed the suspicions of the sergeant and he promptly gave chase and took the offender into custody.

6 FEBRUARY   1922   A fifty-two-year-old man named John Murray was remitted to the Sheriff Court on the charge of throwing a five-year-old boy over the western parapet of the Stockwell Bridge into the Clyde. Murray, who was described as being 'of unkempt and pinched appearance', pleaded not guilty to the crime, which appeared at the time to be motiveless. An ex-soldier, Murray had served in India and had suffered from tuberculosis. On passing the bridge that day, he had seen the boy looking through the balustrade and without any warning, had seized the child and thrown him into the river. Murray later stated that he wanted to commit a crime to get into some kind of home, as he was incurable of his illness and had been poverty stricken and going without food. The boy, who had been coming home from school when the incident happened, was said to have been still clutching his school bag when he was taken out of the water. He was taken to the Royal Infirmary, where he eventually recovered from the ordeal. John Murray was sentenced to three years penal servitude on the 25 February 1922, with the Lord Justice Clerk commenting that 'it was impossible to tolerate such things being done in a civilised country'.

7 FEBRUARY   1845   At the Police Court, two females who were keepers of what were commonly called 'pig's feet shops', were brought before the Magistrate on the charge of having their places of business in New and Old Wynds open for the entertainment of people between the hours of twelve at night and five in the morning, which was contrary to the Police Act. The evidence showed that in one of these houses there were no fewer that fifteen persons, described as 'thieves and disreputable females', having a raucous time and eating pig's feet and potatoes. The women were convicted and fined 10s each. The magistrate commented that 'these houses were a much greater evil to the community than others which were considered to be of a worse description'.

8 FEBRUARY

1855 In a case of 'street begging', a woman described as a 'vagrant' was brought before the Police Court on a charge of being 'found begging, and with being an incorrigible vagrant and common beggar, who refuses to give up her vagrant habits, or to cease begging after being admonished, or required to do so by one or more of the magistrates of Glasgow'. The woman was convicted of this charge and sent back to the town's hospital, which was the local poorhouse, where she had lately been an inmate. A local newspaper at the time commented that it was, 'surely a farce to send such a person back to the Poor's House, when there is no power to compel her to remain. It would not be undue severity to send the worst of these characters to prison for a month or so.'

9 FEBRUARY

1821 A report appeared in the newspapers on this date of a fourteen-year-old boy named Alexander Gollans, described as 'by habit and repute a thief.' Gollans had been taken into custody and imprisoned on a charge of stealing six pairs of shoes. In a state of alarm at his circumstances, the boy attempted to hang himself in the cell with his handkerchief. Luckily, Gollans was found before his young life ended, and was taken down in 'a state of dreadful convulsions'.

10 FEBRUARY

1826 In the Police Court, a woman described as 'an old hag' was found guilty of stealing a shawl and a silk handkerchief from two little girls in Stockwell Street. The woman had enticed the children to give her the articles to hold, while they went up the stair of a close to enquire for a person she pretended to be looking for. The 'old hag' was sentenced to sixty days' imprisonment in the Bridewell.

11 FEBRUARY

1920 Two men and two women suspected of the murder of a man named Henry Senior in Queen's Park Recreation Grounds were brought back to Glasgow on this date, after fleeing to Belfast. A considerable number of people had assembled at Glasgow Central station and when the prisoners appeared, they were subjected to, 'a good deal of booing and hissing'. All four appeared in the Police Court during the course of the morning and were remanded in custody. The charge against them was that whilst they were in the Recreation Ground they assaulted thirty-five-year-old Henry Senior by seizing hold of him and compressing his throat, knocking him down and kicking him. Their intention being to rob Mr Senior, the four then took his overcoat, shoes, pocketbook and a sum of money. He died from his injuries. Having fled to Ireland, the two men had been living in a cave at a public park named Cave Hill, four miles out of Belfast, and had spent the nights in a hayshed at a nearby croft. The two women had remained in Belfast and whilst the men were on their way to meet them there, they were all arrested. The clothing stolen from Mr Senior was discovered by detectives in a Glasgow pawn shop.

12 FEBRUARY   1855   A case of drowning occurred at Pollokshaws, when a young man named Williamson, had arranged to play a game of curling with a few of his fellow workmen at Cowglen Pond. Having no curling stones of his own, Williamson had borrowed a pair, which he had promised to return when the match was over. In order to transport the curling stones from Cowglen back to Pollokshaws, Williamson had borrowed a hand barrow from Mr Hutchison, the gamekeeper.

However, in attempting to shorten the distance, he tried to cross the frozen River Cart, the ice on which, owing to the recent thaw, gave way, sending Williamson to a watery grave. The body was recovered, and on examining his watch, it was discovered that it had stopped at quarter past ten, only half an hour after leaving his workmates.

13 FEBRUARY   1855   A sad story appeared in the newspapers on this date which highlighted the distress existing among the young women engaged in the sewed muslin trade. Two sisters rented a room in a street in the Gorbals; one of them working in a muslin warehouse, the other carrying out the same work at home. However, as was common at the time, the work dried up and the sisters attempted to gain a livelihood by some other means, but failed in their endeavours. If not for the sympathy and assistance of their neighbours, these two women would have very quickly died of starvation. Unfortunately, however, the neighbours could not keep up this assistance and although the lives of the sisters were prolonged, it was only for a time, and they died within twenty-four hours of each other.

The River Clyde.

14 FEBRUARY   **1858**   A fifteen-year-old boy named William Braiden, employed in Tennant's works, St Rollox, was carrying out his work, which included taking charge of a boiler. Tragically, industrial accidents involving children being all too common at this time, the boiler burst and the boy was severely scalded, later dying in the infirmary. Eventually in the late 1860s, the Factory Act was introduced in an attempt to improve conditions for children working in factories, and set a minimum age for child workers and maximum amount of hours they could work depending on their age.

15 FEBRUARY   **1857**   A 'dangerous case of insanity' was reported on this date. While the steamer *Lapwing* was on her passage from Inverness to Clyde, one of the passengers, named Alexander Campbell, was said to have 'become perfectly insane', and attempted to stab the captain and several of the crew with a penknife. Campbell, on appearing in front of the magistrate, stated that he was a Sheriff Officer in Inverness and that he had business in the city. His manner, however, described as 'wild and unconnected', left the authorities in no doubt of his insanity.

16 FEBRUARY

1821 In another sad case of an industrial accident, a fifteen-year-old boy was employed in oiling the shafts of an engine, when one of his arms became entangled in the machinery and was torn off above the elbow. He was immediately taken to the infirmary, and due to the shattered state of the bones in his upper arm, amputation from the shoulder was performed. The boy's ribs had also been broken and as a result of all the injuries sustained, he died a few days later. Children were often used for cleaning and maintenance jobs in factories, as due to their small size, they could fit into places in the machinery that the men could not access. This by its very nature, was a perilous practice for the boys and frequently ended in tragedy.

17 FEBRUARY

1820 The following article appeared in the *Glasgow Herald* newspaper, highlighting the social conditions in Glasgow at this time:

> In a small corner of this city, containing 229 families, no less than 109 grown up persons are unable to read, and these are found to be chiefly parents. The result of ignorance is generally a disregard to every moral obligation, and the announcement that out of that number, 163 families are without seats in any place of worship, may enable the public to form their own conclusions with regard to the character of such people in such circumstances. If parents are ignorant and immoral; what can be hoped for from their offspring? Laws may check, and justice may be, and we believe is, most impartially and conscientiously administered; but it must be confessed to be little more than throwing a mangle of obscurity over a body diseased; whilst the root and origin remain untouched and unattended to. Were the foregoing district the only one so deplorable, less anxiety might be necessary to effect the cure, but when it is found to be but a small portion of a yet unexplored mass of poverty and ignorance, surely the latent energies of every Christian ought to be roused to their fullest extent.

18 FEBRUARY

Areas of Glasgow – Bridgeton

Bridgeton was a district in the east of Glasgow, next to Glasgow Green, Dalmarnock and Calton. Beginning as a small weaving district on the lands at Goosefauld, the area of Bridgeton, after the construction of the Rutherglen Bridge across the River Clyde in 1775, got its name after becoming known as the 'Bridge Town'. In the early days of Bridgeton, there was very much lacking in the way of sanitation, with a cleansing contractor being employed to sweep the streets only six times a year. Additionally, pavements were virtually unknown until around 1830, and buckets of waste were thrown out of houses on to the street. Persons walking along the street would often have to be on their guard for the human waste coming out of the front doors of houses there. In a report on the 'Measures adopted in conformity with the special regulations of the General Board of Health' in 1849, sanitation in the area of Bridgeton was described:

These places consist of ranges of narrow closes, only some four or five feet in width, and of great length. The houses are so lofty, that the direct light of the sky never reaches a large proportion of the dwellings. There are large square middensteads, some of them actually under the houses and all of them in the immediate vicinity of the windows and doors of human dwellings. These receptacles hold the entire filth and offal of large masses of people and households, until country farmers can be bargained with for their removal. There is no drainage in these neighbourhoods, except in a few cases; and from the want of any means of flushing, the sewers, where they do exist, are extended cesspools polluting the air. So little is the use of sewers known, that on one occasion I saw the entire surface of a back yard covered for several inches with green putrid water, although there was a sewer in the close within a few feet, into which it might have been drained away. The water supply is also very defective; such a thing as a household supply is unknown, and I have been informed that from the state of the law, the Water Companies find it impossible to recover rates, and that, had the cholera not appeared, it was in contemplation to have cut off the entire supply from this class of property ... There are no domestic conveniences even in the loftiest tenements, where they are most needed, except a kind of wooden sink placed outside some stair window, and communicating by a square wooden pipe with the surface of the close or court beneath. Down this contrivance, where it does exist, is poured the entire filth of the household or flat to which it belongs, and the solid refuse not infrequently takes the same direction till the tube becomes obstructed.

19 FEBRUARY   **1924** The Glasgow Police on this date reported the death of Robert Rankin, the thirteen-month-old child of Joseph Rankin, a fish salesman. Before going out for groceries, the child's mother had placed him in bed, putting pillows in front of him to prevent him falling out. However, when she returned she found the child suspended head downwards by his nightdress from an iron pillar of a crib which was standing in front of the bed.

20 FEBRUARY **1909** The case of a shooting in the Hillhead area of Glasgow was reported on this date. On a previous night, a man of about forty years of age called at a house in Hillhead Street and asked to see the occupier. When she came to the door the man asked her where his wife was. On being informed that she was not in the house, the man proceeded to interrogate the lady as to the movements of his wife, who it is reported, had previously been in the service of the lady. After asking the man to go away, the lady attempted to close the door, when the man drew a revolver from his pocked and fired point blank at her. However, the lady, who had suspected the man's motive, jumped to one side and escaped uninjured. The man then ran down the stairs and escaped, but was arrested later in a close in Gairbraid Street, Maryhill and charged with attempted murder.

21 FEBRUARY **1845** As the 7 a.m. train from Glasgow was approaching the old Kirkintilloch station, a passenger in one of the open carriages lost his hat after it was blown off in the wind. Being under the influence of alcohol at the time, he attempted to open the door of the carriage to get out and retrieve it, but was prevented by doing so by the other passengers. Determined, however, the man threw himself over the side of the carriage and continued to hold on by the buffer end until the train was passing the disused station, when he relinquished his grasp and tried to get a footing upon the platform there. Due to the speed the train was going, however, the man was thrown down with great force and was considerably injured about the face and head.

22 FEBRUARY **1846** A young shoe cleaner by the name of Daniel Brown, was charged in the Police Court with having 'attempted to impose on several gentlemen, by presenting a certificate purporting to be signed by James Lumsden, Esq. Lord Provost, and William Gilmour, Esq. of Oatlands, setting forth the destitute character of the bearer, and recommending him to the charitable consideration of the public'. Brown pleaded guilty to the charge and was sentenced to sixty days' imprisonment. The Scottish Poor Law Act of 1845 had led to the establishment of parochial boards in the parishes and towns. However, mismanagement of this system resulted in a more restricted system after 1868 which relied more on the poorhouse.

23 FEBRUARY **1821** In a sad accident at one of the public works in the city, a man was reported to have drunk, instead of water, a quantity of the liquor used in the dyeing process, and in spite of prompt medical aid, he only survived for a few days. The man left a widow and several children.

24 FEBRUARY **1848** McKellar, a messenger at arms, along with an assistant, apprehended a man named Docherty on a charge of debt. However, as they were conveying him to prison from his residence in Rose Street and walking unsuspectingly along Crown Street, they were approached by a number of men, one of whom suddenly aimed a blow at McKellar and struck him so severely behind the ear that he was knocked down. With the motive of the attack being to rescue the prisoner out of the hands of the officers, Docherty took full advantage of the diversion and ran off, but was caught by a constable named Price. The group of men, seeing that Docherty had again been caught, turned their attention to Price, attempting to tear the prisoner from him. Price's grip, however, was so strong that Docherty was knocked down along with him in the struggle. After giving the constable several violent kicks on the head and sides, the men then succeeded in liberating Docherty by cutting the cloth which the constable had hold of. The party then ran away, but a few of them, having been recognised in the scuffle, were apprehended in the course of the evening.

25 FEBRUARY **1820** During the night, the gardener at a large house on the outskirts of the city, was alarmed by the barking of the watch dog. Taking a loaded gun, he went outside to check the area. On reaching the poultry house, however, a man rushed out of the door and threw a quantity of powder in his face, which rendered him totally blind and considerably burned.

26 FEBRUARY **1850** A gentleman who entered a hotel at the foot of Jamaica Street, late the previous evening, partook of some refreshments and shortly afterwards retired to bed. In the early hours of the morning, a guest in the adjoining room heard a loud noise like that of a pistol, but thinking the noise had came from outside, paid no attention to it. By the afternoon, as the gentleman had not emerged from his room, the servant was sent to wake him. Finding no response to her calls at the door, she entered the room and saw a pistol lying on the floor and the unfortunate man with a wound on his forehead bleeding profusely. Medical aid was immediately called, and the wound dressed. His friends, on finding out about the

Jamaica Street, around the turn of the century.

occurrence, stated that he had only recently recovered from an attack of typhus fever, which in the absence of any other motive, was thought to have accounted for the suicide attempt.

27 FEBRUARY   **Areas of Glasgow – Anderston**

Situated on the north bank of the River Clyde, Anderston was an independent burgh until 1846, when it was incorporated into the City of Glasgow. Originally a small village, developed on the land of James Anderson, the area was named 'Anderson Town' in his honour, later becoming known as Anderston. The Gushet farm next to the area, became known as Anderston Cross, and is the site of the Kingston Bridge today. In the early to mid-eighteenth century, Anderston had bleachfields down by the river and weavers' cottages lined the Main Street. The size of Anderston increased as business in the area grew, becoming an established industrial centre with the growth of several industries in Glasgow including the cotton industry. The area was originally popular with Irish immigrants, and by the early nineteenth century was a thriving community, with most of the people living there employed in the many industries. Inevitably, however, this rapid development of industry led to demand for working-class housing, and in the late nineteenth century,

Anderston Cross.

solid stone tenement buildings, well known in Glasgow, were built to deal with the overcrowding. Cases of fever had been particularly prevalent in this area, due to the overcrowding and inevitable unsanitary conditions that followed. In 1848, a letter to the editor of the *Glasgow Herald* from a slightly unsympathetic Glasgow resident spoke of the state of housing in this area:

> There is a large tenement in Anderson which, for a number of years past, has been chiefly inhabited by paupers. From this peculiarity of occupancy it has received the title of 'poors house'. It has, however, other claims to this distinction. He would be a very acute observer that would discover one whole pane of glass in the extensive square of houses of which this beggars lodge is composed. In most tenements, where breaches of this kind occur, some substitute is generally found, such as an old hat or a bunch of dirty rags, which, though not so transparent as the glaziers invaluable article, nor adding little in the way of ornament to the architecture of the buildings, indicates at least that the house is inhabited by some other vitality than rats and mice. But here the bare and vacant casement alone adorns the walls and in some cases, there is only a fragment of it ... But if the exterior of the building presents so many remarkable features, the interior of one of the houses which

I entered beggars description. It is like Shakespeare's picture of old age; it abounds in negatives – 'sans eyes, sans teeth, sans taste, sans everything'. So this house – sans beds, sans shelves, sans chairs, sans everything. All that would burn or pawn has vanished The very doors have been torn off their hinges and used for fuel.

28 FEBRUARY

1890   In court on this date, a case described as 'a typical Bridgegate case' was heard. The case featured a woman and two men accused of robbing a labourer, Thomas O'Brien, of 7s 6d and a hat. O'Brien stated that he was under the railway bridge in Bridgegate when he was struck on the chest by the female prisoner, and this blow was followed by another on the side of his chest by one of the male prisoners. The other male prisoner had then joined in and O'Brien, being overpowered, was robbed. He also stated that on the morning of the trial, he had been offered money to stop the case. The counsel for the accused, attempting to discredit O'Brien, asked him, 'Are you a Protestant or a Roman Catholic?', to which he replied, 'I am a Roman Catholic.'

Lord Shand, presiding, then interjected, 'My experience of Roman Catholics is that they are as truthful as any other people.'

The trial continued and Constable Alston gave evidence that, on approaching the scene of the robbery, a struggle ensued in which he was knocked down.

Lord Shand asked the constable, 'Don't they help the police in the Bridgegate on occasions like this?'

Constable Alston replied, 'It is a singular occasion if they do, my Lord.'

The jury, by a majority, found the three prisoners guilty.

29 FEBRUARY

1924   On this date, the case of an 'Italian Shopkeeper Found Shot Dead' was reported. Fortunato Fattori, a sixty-four-year-old man, who resided at 575 Argyle Street, was found dead the previous afternoon in the back portion of his business premises at 6 North Street. It was reported that Antonio Fattori, 27, who assisted in the business, had been sent on an errand to a neighbouring shop at the time by his father. On returning three or four minutes later, he found the back shop full of smoke and his father lying in the corner. Medical aid was summoned, but he was found to be dead. A double-barrelled gun containing an empty cartridge case was found near the body. It was thought that Fortunato Fattori had been worried owing to recent dull trade and had therefore committed suicide.

MARCH

Selling from barrows in Glasgow, early twentieth century.

1 MARCH

1852 A case of the 'theft of pauper clothes' was heard before the sheriff. Sarah Kelly was charged with running away from the Poorhouse of Glasgow, where she was an inmate, and taking with her a petticoat and shift, which were the property of the Parochial Board, and pawning them for money. Kelly was found guilty and sentenced to ten days' imprisonment. Poorhouses, public institutions which housed and fed people who were unable to support themselves, were intended to be hostile and harsh places in which only the truly destitute would seek refuge. It was hoped that the poorhouses would solve the problem of poverty as many rich people believed people were poor because they were lazy and referred to them as the 'undeserving poor'.

2 MARCH

1845 Anthony McCormick, a woolcarder, was charged at the Police Court with 'assaulting, kicking and striking' Janet McLachlan, a worker in the same factory. From the evidence it appeared that the accused was a foreman in charge of the girl, and that this violent assault had been his method of correcting her for some imperfection in her work. It also emerged that in consequence of reporting the assault, Janet McLachlan had been dismissed from the factory. McCormick was found guilty and fined 20s.

3 MARCH

1826 Two young fleshers were charged on this date with 'barbarously setting a dog upon a servant girl'. This incident had taken place whilst the girl was drying clothes in Glasgow Green, and resulted in a deep incision being made in her leg by the dog's teeth. They were found guilty and fined three guineas, half of which was to be given to the servant girl.

4 MARCH

1802 Janet McLellan, keeper of a tambouring work in the Drygate, and widow of James McLellan, appeared in the Council Chamber in consequence of a summons given to her to pay an outstanding fine. The fine given to Mrs McLellan was for 'exercising the most atrocious cruelties' upon an orphan girl named Agnes Livingston, who was employed in her service. By the evidence given, it had been previously proven that Mrs McLellan, her neice and two other girls in her service had burned the girl on almost every part of her body with red hot tongs, held the soles of her feet to the grate, lashed her with a knotted rope and a horsewhip, and put brine upon the wounds to make them hurt more. All this was carried out under the pretence that she was letting her work fall behind. The poor girl had finally made her escape one day and on being admitted to the Infirmary of Glasgow, the magistrates were made aware of the crimes.

5 MARCH   1856 At the River Bailie Court, H.K. Mainwaring, master of a ship, and Marcus Fenner, mate of the same ship, were brought up on a charge of assault. The ship had arrived in the harbour about a fortnight prior to this date, and on the previous weekend five of the crew had been employed in carrying pig iron on board the ship, four of whom paired up in order to carry the heavier pieces between them, leaving the fifth person, a lad named Connell, to carry the smaller pieces on his own. However, the master ordered Connell to take one of the heavier pieces, which he twice attempted to do, but he was unable to bear the weight of it.

The master angrily seized Connell and pushed him into the cabin and, with the assistance of the mate, handcuffed him. The mate afterwards, by the master's instructions, put Connell into the main hold and fastened him by a rope around his wrists, to one of the stanchions, keeping him in a stooping posture for about an hour. In the meantime, the police had been notified by one of the other crew as to what was going on and Detective McLachlan arrived at the ship. On seeing Connell, he ordered him to be released and the rope was removed. It was some time before the removal of the handcuffs, however, as the master had gone ashore, carrying the key in his pocket. The two men were found guilty of the charge, with the master being fined three guineas, and the mate, one guinea.

6 MARCH   1814 A 'melancholy accident' was reported on this date, involving the collapse of a building in Saltmarket Street. On a previous afternoon, the north wall of the south wing of a large house in Saltmarket Street, suddenly gave way and fell into the close with a tremendous crash. The principal part of the five storeys, occupied by nine families, and offices situated above, instantaneously collapsed into a heap of debris, with a number of the inhabitants buried in the ruins. The cries of the buried inhabitants could be heard coming from the rubble. A crowd of people who had formed began to give assistance and ladders were obtained to reach some of the occupants. One of the buried inhabitants, a woman, could not be found. The fall of the house was attributed to alterations that were being made in the ground floor, and several families,

fearing for the safety of the building, had fortunately moved out earlier in the day.

7 MARCH

Glasgow Institutions – Glasgow Royal Infirmary

Opened in 1794, the hospital is situated at the head of the city's medieval High Street. Originally having a capacity of 136, an extension in 1815 gave the hospital a bed capacity of 208, with a separate 220-bed fever house added in 1828 to cope with the city's fever outbreaks which were prevalent at the time, and continued throughout the century. A letter from a Glasgow resident to the editor of the *Glasgow Herald* in 1869 comments on the fever problem in the city:

> On reading the report of the Police Board in the Herald this morning, I was very much astonished and grieved to find that the cases of fever during the last two weeks, as reported by Dr Gairdner, occuring in this city, were at the alarming number of nearly 150 per week, or for two weeks, 291 cases; and that there were on 2 December last 130 patients in the fever hospital at the expense of Police funds. This state of matters is most distressing, and loudly demands instant attention on the part of our Police authorities. As a ratepayer and citizen, I have a right to know what is being done by our Police and Sanitary officers in the way of prevention. It is all very well to provide hospital accommodation and medical attendance for fever patients; but I hold that prevention is better than cure, and some more energetic measures must be adopted without delay to prevent the further spreading of this fatal disease … For instance, I learn that in many places out of which fever patients were taken, other people are allowed to remain, without the infected houses being properly cleansed or fumigated. Could not in every case the people be removed for a few days to some temporary asylum, and the infected beds and clothes taken care of, so that these are properly cleansed or burnt at the public expense, and examination also made as to the cause of the fever in the house or tenement where it may occur?

A lack of cleanliness and sanitation in dwellings, and the subsequent infections caused were often responsible for a drain on hospital resources, and in fact, hospitals themselves were often not the sterile places we know today. However, a new Surgical House opened in 1861, in which Joseph Lister, the pioneer of antiseptics, later developed his use of carbolic acid in cleaning instruments and washing hands before and after surgery, revolutionising surgical procedures. Additionally, a student of Lister, William MacEwen, on becoming a full surgeon at the hospital in 1877, introduced the practice of doctors wearing white coats which could be sterilised. Prior to these advancements, it had been more common for patients to die from infection caused by the unhygienic conditions in which the surgical procedure would take place, than to die from the original ailment.

8 MARCH

1931 Thomas Beggs, thirty-eight years old, appeared in Glasgow Sheriff Court on this date charged with murder. The charge had been changed from assault to murder, as the victim, his wife, had died in the Western Infirmary from her injuries. In their house at 20 Hastie Street, Overnewton, Beggs had assaulted his wife Marion, by striking her on the head with a hammer. Beggs' submitted a special defence of temporary insanity at the time of the offence. The case was remitted in the High Court of Glasgow, where midway through the trial the court accepted a plea of guilty to culpable homicide.

Evidence given at the trial by Beggs' son, also Thomas Beggs, was that there were frequent quarrels between his father and stepmother, which mainly arose through Mrs Beggs taunting his father about his inability to find work. On one occasion, the boy stated, his stepmother tried to stab his father with a knife. On the night of the incident, young Thomas Beggs awoke during the night after hearing noises like 'cracks' coming from the kitchen. There he found his stepmother lying with blood streaming from her head. He spoke to her but she could not answer him. Young Beggs ran downstairs to summon the police but saw his father on the corner of the street, who beckoned him towards him. Young Thomas asked his father why he had done it, to which his father did not reply, only stating that he had 'did it with a hammer'. Other witnesses gave evidence of seeing Thomas Beggs senior after the incident and described him as looking 'wild and excited' and 'like a madman'. One witness, Joseph Park, said that Beggs told him he had 'finished her

this time'. At the end of the proceedings, he was sentenced to three years' penal servitude.

9 MARCH

1846 David Finlayson, a carter, while passing along Malta Street in the Gorbals with a horse and cart laden with coals, came into contact with a ten-year-old girl. The girl was knocked down by the cart and the wheels passed over her body. She was taken home and a surgeon was called in. The girl later miraculously recovered from the incident.

10 MARCH

1845 A woman, the wife of a rat catcher, was charged in the Police Court with having sent out her five-year-old child to beg. The child had been found on the street and taken charge of by the police. On ascertaining the identity of the child's parents, the police attempted to return her to her mother. However, the girl screamed and held on to the nurse who had been looking after her. With it being apparent that there must be some reason for the girl to so reluctant to return home, further enquiries were made. When the child's mother appeared in court, the child again began to cry and held on to the nursemaid. Mr Willox, the inspector of the city poor agreed to let the child remain with her present guardian and pay for her keep, rather than send her back to the 'unnatural parents'.

11 MARCH

1844 Foreman in a wadding manufacturers, Alexander Gillespie, met his death in what was described as 'a very shocking manner'.

He was greasing the main shaft of the steam engine, when some part of his clothing became caught by a belt, and he was drawn up to the roof of the engine room with such force, it was reported, that 'his head was literally smashed to pieces.'

12 MARCH   1844   Six young thieves who had been cutting the glass of shopkeepers' windows in the Gorbals and inserting a piece of wire with a crook at the end of it to draw out goods, were caught red handed on this date. The young men had been carrying out this practice for some time in the area.

13 MARCH   1854   At the Police Court, Daniel McGuire, a young boy, was accused of having assaulted another boy, named Edward McSally, in the High Street with a knife on the previous day. It seems that several of the 'young delinquents of the High Street' had been amusing themselves in the afternoon, when McGuire became exasperated at the conduct of some of the boys, who had been annoying him. He threatened that the first boy who came near him would be stabbed, and he took a knife from his pocket. McSally at this point rushed up to McGuire, who proceeded to stab him in the arm. The magistrate in this case sentenced McGuire, described as 'a young blackguard', to twenty-five lashes, a common punishment for youth crime in this era.

14 MARCH   1851   A case of 'contemptible conduct' was heard at the Gorbals Police Court. Two young men, one a baker and the other a ship's carpenter, were charged with 'wantonly and maliciously' decoying another young man, James Croall, described as 'a silly lad', into a public house, where they plied him with alcohol. Once Croall was sufficiently drunk, the two boys, for their own amusement, proceeded to cut off all of his hair. In doing this however, they also managed to cut a piece out of Croall's ear. They were found guilty and fined two guineas each.

15 MARCH   Glasgow Institutions – HMP Barlinnie
Due to overcrowding in Duke Street Prison and Glasgow Green Prison, the decision was taken to build a new four-block prison, which could house 200 prisoners in each block. Land was purchased in 1879 from the Barlinnie Farm Estate, consisting of 32.5 acres, and building work began in 1880. It is reported that the oldest part of the current health centre building predates the jail, as this was the farm

manager's office and residence. HMP Barlinnie first became a place of legal detention in 1882, with A Hall receiving its first prisoners on 25 July that year. Prisoners were used for labouring work, including quarrying and breaking stone, to facilitate the building of the other three halls, each of which opened as soon as it was completed. The number of prisoners, however, exceeded all expectations and an additional hall was built in 1893, following the extension of the perimeter wall. Overcrowding was still a feature of the prison even after these extensions, with the additional problem of short staffing. A letter to the editor of the *Glasgow Herald* in 1899 highlighted the problem:

> With the evil of understaffing and short handedness ... no consideration is shown to the shorthanded warder staffs who are, and have been, systematically overworked, doubtless without the knowledge of the Secretary for Scotland, and without all hope of redress from a hard and grinding administrative bureau. This is another subject calling urgently for a public inquiry into Scotch prisons. There is constant discontent and dissatisfaction throughout the Scottish prison service, a prevalent atmosphere of suspicion, and a total want of confidence.

16 MARCH

1846   An article in the *Glasgow Herald* highlights the conditions in the suburb of Bridgeton, stating:

> All that we should require to prove to any one, absolutely necessary for the supervision by police in Bridgeton, would be an hour's look at the place, at the streets, the closes, the ash pits etc. It is a positive wonder that disease is not engendered to a much larger degree than it is by the accumulations of filth which are heaped up from month to month on the public streets, and which choke up the closes and passages. This is one glaring evil to be remedied, but the greatest of all is the bold and daring commission of crime, even in broad daylight, which goes unpunished. The peaceable inhabitants are in constant terror, and the grossest delinquencies are perpetrated by the most contemptible fellows with impunity. As a sample of what is common, it may be mentioned that the most respectable and influential of the inhabitants are afraid to interfere, even when the merest youths are the aggressors – and that within a few months there has been numerous housebreakings and

robberies – people have been all but murdered by mobs of colliers – the Sabbath mornings have been generally devoted to fighting – and the smashing of windows is common – four shops were lately broken open in one night – a trick of the worthless is to go into spirit cellars, drink their fill, and walk off without paying – there are constant fightings betwixt men and their wives – and thefts of rails and metal from doors is of nightly occurrence; indeed, all sorts of delinquencies are frequent; some of them of the most daring description. On Sunday eight days, a great number of thieves and bad characters from the Calton commenced a regular row, and amused themselves by knocking down all the respectable persons who passed. The crowd at length amounted to two or three hundred, and there was no assistance to be had. Last Monday, one of the natives amused himself during the forenoon in shooting at a mark across one of the principal streets; and a short time ago, while a wedding party were engaged up stairs, the coach and horses, which had been left at the door, were run off with! We could add a hundred items to the catalogue, but we suppose this is enough to prove our case.

17 MARCH   **1848**   A case was reported in the newspapers on this date with the heading 'Matrimonial Felicity'. On a previous night, about eleven o'clock, the inhabitants of Canning Street, Calton, were alarmed by screams of 'murder', coming from the house of a weaver named Hanning. Police assistance was obtained and on entering the house from which the noise came, they ascertained that the weaver was in a state of intoxication and was striking his wife. When they attempted to take him into custody, a struggle ensued which resulted in the lamps carried by the policemen being smashed to pieces. Hanning had been frequently convicted of similar offences and severely fined, but all too often his wife would come forward and pay the fine for him. On this occasion though, she allowed the law to take its course and the weaver was sentenced to sixty days' imprisonment.

18 MARCH   **1850**   A person employed at a works in Monkland which manufactured bar iron, whilst engaged about the machinery, became entangled among a portion of it, and was dragged between the large rollers through which the iron passed. His body, as would be expected, was terribly mangled and he died half an hour afterwards.

19 MARCH   **1865** In the parish of Old Monkland, Police Constable Neil McKay, was attacked and viciously assaulted outside the house of spirit dealer Mark Kennedy. Constable McKay had been passing by around midnight when he heard noise coming from the back of the spirit shop. Upon further investigation, he found five men at the back of the premises, kicking at the door. The men grabbed hold of the constable, and he was punched, kicked, hit with a stick, dragged to the railway bridge, and pushed over the bridge. The five men accused of the assault were later sentenced to twelve months' imprisonment each.

20 MARCH   **1848** On this morning, a labourer named Donald Cameron, residing on this in McAlpine Street, who had been 'indulging freely in alcohol', was sitting at his fireside smoking, when his wife, who was in bed, asked him for a light. Cameron complied with this request by throwing her a piece of lighted paper. His wife, insulted at this cavalier treatment, retaliated by throwing the paper back again. Unfortunately, the paper fell short of its intended destination, going through a hole in the floor and landing on a quantity of straw and shavings which had been placed between the beams of the floor. In a moment, the place had become ablaze and the whole neighbourhood was in a state of panic. Buckets of water were quickly obtained, however, and the fire was confined to the apartment in which it originated. Following the incident, Cameron, not relishing the prospect of a police cell, resisted determinedly with the constable who had been called for, and attempted to throw the constable out of one of the windows. Having finally been taken to the police office, he was sentenced in the Police Court to twenty days' imprisonment.

21 MARCH   **1853** Shortly after ten o'clock in the morning, neighbours heard cries from the home of Robert Paton, a carpet weaver in Canal Street, Tradeston. Paton's six-year-old daughter Lavinia, who had been left alone in the house, had become engulfed in flames, her clothes having caught alight from the fire. On the door being forced open by the neighbours, her body was discovered lying on the floor, blackened by the flames. Robert Paton had also been afflicted by a series of other calamities in the five years prior to this incident, having lost his wife and other daughter to typhus fever; his son dying from swallowing poison; another son drowning while bathing and Paton himself recently breaking his leg.

22 MARCH

Areas of Glasgow – Calton

North of the River Clyde, Calton was a Burgh of Barony from 1817 to 1846, after which it became part of the City of Glasgow. From the eighteenth century, the area had become known for its weaving industry, an industry in which workers were seeing reductions in their wages due to cheaper textiles starting to be imported from overseas. Many disputes, often of a violent nature, arose between workers who decided to strike and those who carried on working for the lower wages. In the twentieth century, the area became well known for its Barras Street market and Barrowland Ballroom. Throughout the nineteenth century, however, the area had experienced sectarian tensions following large numbers of people moving to the area from Ireland, combined with poverty and other social problems. In 1851 the population was over 36,000, creating inevitably, a large amount of deprivation and poverty with people living in slum conditions rife with disease. A report in the *Glasgow Herald* in 1846 noted that, 'Little hope can be entertained of effectually raising the moral character and physical condition of the great bulk of our population, till something is done to improve their dwellings'.

23 MARCH

1821 A thirteen-year-old boy, described by many as 'a fine boy', suffered a fatal accident whilst working in the Cowglen Coal Pit. Standing at the bottom of the pit, he was hit on the head by a piece of coal which fell from an ascending hutch, and was killed on the spot.

24 MARCH

1826 A novel type of theft was committed in Drygate Street. Whilst a shopkeeper was giving 10s of change to a customer, a large stick, dipped in tar and held by a person outside the door, came down upon the money with such force as to startle everyone in the shop. The stick was instantly withdrawn, and along with it 5s 6d of the change, which stuck to the tar. The people were so astounded by this act, that the thief was clear away before they could recollect themselves.

25 MARCH

1844 At about fifteen minutes past four o'clock, five-year-old Charles Murray was killed at the west end of Cowcaddens. The young boy had left the Infant School of the Normal Seminary, along with the rest of the children and was attempting to cross the road when he was knocked down by one of the horses, with one of the wheels of the coach passing over his head. The driver of the 'Enterprise', as it was called, was said to have called out to the children, but five-year-old Charles did not hear him. It was reported in the papers that these coaches were 'frequently driven very rapidly'. This had been the second tragedy to have befallen the boy's family, with his brother having died the previous week.

26 MARCH **1847** A report of a 'riot in the Gorbals' appeared in the newspapers on this date. The previous Sunday, as the churches were emptying after service, a disturbance took place at the head of Main Street, Gorbals. Two men, described as 'blackguards', had commenced a fight on the street, when the police intervened. On seeing this, two workmen came forward to rescue the men who were being taken into custody. During this time, a 'considerable commotion' was taking place, with a crowd of people and some of the police were severely injured. The result of this had been that the original two made their escape and the two men who had assisted them were taken into custody. After their trial, they were both convicted and sentenced to thirty days' imprisonment.

27 MARCH **1861** Archibald Finlay, a teacher, appeared in the Police Court accused of having assaulted nine-year-old Isabella Donald in the Industrial Schoolroom. Finlay was said to have struck Isabella several violent blows with a leather strap on her back, shoulders and arms. From the evidence given, it seemed that the girl had been attending the school for eight days and on the day of the incident, she had failed to properly learn a task that she had been given. Finlay ordered her to hold out her hand to receive punishment, but Isabella had hesitated, upon which Finlay became angry and hit her with the strap until her back and shoulders were 'black and blue'. Finlay was convicted and fined the sum of £5. The purpose of Industrial Schools was to develop the potential of the more destitute children, who were at risk of becoming involved in crime, and to give them a good work ethic, by providing them with discipline, education and teaching them a trade. Many of the children who ended up in these schools had been homeless.

28 MARCH **1853** An article appeared in the *Glasgow Herald*, on the crime of garrotting:

Scarceley a day or night passes over without some startling account of the cool and deliberate perpetration of this crime in Glasgow.

A Cat-o'-nine-tails.

It recalls to our recollection the horrid practice of vitriol throwing in this city many years ago. Every means of punishment had been tried to check that brutal enormity, but in vain. At last, Lord Meadowbank came to Glasgow, and he hit upon a punishment which checked and ended it most effectively. He ordered the guilty culprit to be stripped from the shoulders – to be taken to the gibbet, the public place of execution in front of the jail, and there to receive so many lashes from the hands of the executioner with the cat-o'-nine-tails; and then to be tied to a cart, and receive so many additional stripes at particular places on the public streets. After that was done, the squirting of vitriol on innocent people ceased in Glasgow. It was never more heard of. But we have so many humanity mongers in Glasgow nowadays that even the laudable attempts to repress crime are frequently baffled. Let the first convicted band of garrotters at the Circuit Court in Glasgow meet the fate which Kane, the vitriol thrower, received, and we are mistaken if the same results will not follow.

Cases of 'garrotting', were common in this period. This was a crime typically carried out by street ruffians and involved strangling the victim from behind in order to commit robbery. This type of crime caused panic amongst the public, particularly amongst the better off residents, as the victims were usually gentlemen. Protective collars could be purchased which were made of steel and studded with sharp spikes, which could be worn around the neck to deter the garrotters.

29 MARCH   1853   A fourteen-year-old boy named Alexander Clark was severely injured in Exchange Square, in consequence of the bursting of a bottle of nitric acid which he was carrying. He was on his way from the Apothecary Hall, Virginia Street, to the shop of his employer, Mr Cowpar, spirit merchant, West Nile Street, with the acid, when the bottle by some means burst, destroying a portion of his clothing and severely burning his face.

30 MARCH   1822   In the morning, a middle-aged woman, described as being 'in a state of insanity', jumped into the Clyde near the Humane Society House. She had no sooner jumped in, when she changed her mind and made every effort in her power to get out of the water. Fortunately

The River Clyde, near Kirn.

for her, 'some gentlemen' were walking on the banks at the time and one of them handed her an umbrella, which she managed to get hold of and was pulled out. The woman stated that she would not try such an act again, commenting that 'drowning was no better than it was called'.

31 MARCH

1821 Two boys, Daniel Hamilton and Daniel Sinclair, ten years old and nine years old respectively, left school at the usual hour. Instead of going home, however, they wandered down to the south side of the Clyde. On approaching the Inchinnan Bridge, the toll keeper asked them where they were going, to which Sinclair, who had formerly been in the Highlands, said they were on their way there. He advised them to return as they were on the wrong road and the boys accordingly turned around with the intention of getting home before dark. However, nightfall came quicker than they expected and now very weary, the boys lay down by the side of a hedge to rest and fell asleep. They were found the next morning, clasped in each other's arms, with their books lying by their side. Sinclair was dead and Hamilton was 'in a state of insensibility'. Sinclair, described as 'uncommonly stout and healthy for his years', had been warmly dressed, but when found, his clothes had been completely drenched with rain. The damp clothes and sleeping in the open air in a wet cold night was thought to be the cause of his death.

APRIL

Buchanan Street, Glasgow.

1 APRIL

1847 At High Possil, about three miles to the north of Glasgow, Mr Graham, the proprietor of coal works, kept a store in which a quantity of gunpowder used for blasting was kept. The assistant on the premises, a young boy, was engaged in closing the store for the night when a spark from the candle came into contact with the powder, which immediately exploded, resulting in the roof being blown off and the windows forced out. The young assistant was so severely injured that he died a few minutes after his body was recovered from amongst the rubble.

2 APRIL

1847 In the Gorbals Police Court, the case of 'an Irish vagrant caught in a chimney' was heard. Twenty-year-old Mark Martin, described as 'a raw, uncouth Irishman', was charged with having 'illegally and unwarrantably' entered the dwelling house of a victualler in Muirhouse Toll, by going down one of the vents. At about four o'clock on the morning in question, the victualler and his wife, as they lay in bed, were disturbed by a noise in the chimney. As the noise which was growing louder, appeared different from the usual sounds of a burning flue, the couple got out of bed to investigate. To their astonishment, a pair of bare feet and legs were protruding down the chimney in such a position to leave no doubt that the body to which they belonged was there also. The police were promptly summoned and the man handed over to them. On being asked by the magistrate how he accounted for being found in such a situation, the prisoner answered that, 'he was hungry and had gone in search of something to eat', stating, 'sure I didn't know which was the right entrance!'. The court noted, however, that he had taken the precaution to throw off his shoes and stockings, and leave them outside the house prior to descending the chimney, therefore no doubt could be entertained as to his motive. Martin was sentenced to thirty days' imprisonment.

3 APRIL

1846 A report appeared in the *Glasgow Herald* on this date, featuring the subject of Industrial Schools:

> The youths, whom it is proposed shall be taken under charge of the parochial boards, are ranked under three classes. First, those who have been convicted of crime and have been in prison, but are now found wandering the streets as idle vagrants; second, those who have not been convicted nor in prison, but are associates of the first class, and known to the police as having no lawful employment,

and no visible means of support; third, youths not so degraded as either of these two classes, but who, from the poverty or neglect of parents or other relatives, get little or no food, and no education whatever. It is desirable that these three classes should be kept in separate schools; and coming as they all do under the designation of either 'permanent' or 'occasional poor', they are entitled, under the authority of the Poor Law Act, to be educated and supplied with food, clothes, and lodgings at the cost of the parish where settlement has been proved

4 APRIL

1851   At about nine o'clock in the morning, the residents of a house owned by a man named Donaldson, in Greyfriar's Wynd, entered an inner apartment and found their fellow lodger suspended from a bed post by a rope twisted round his neck. The deceased tenant was known as McMillan, a carrier, described as being 'addicted to habits of intemperance' which had led to him losing his job.

5 APRIL

1844   The inhabitants of Calton became aware on this date of a report of a boy named John McLean at 14 Tobago Street, nearly ending his life by hanging himself. His younger brother gave a report that John had climbed upon a chair, fastened a rope to a nail in the wall, then passed the loop around his neck and threw himself from the chair. The cries of the younger boy on seeing this, had brought assistance. Drs Campbell, Young and Donald soon attended, but by this time the boy was cold and no pulse could be detected. However, it occurred to Dr Campbell that this was a good case for trying the effects of electromagnetism, which was popular at the time. Accordingly, a battery with an electromagnetic coil, which Dr Campbell had with him, was put in operation. At first only convulsive breathing started, followed by sighing and crying, then after two hours, the boy sat up and seemed to have returned to normal. When the boy was questioned as to what had made him attempt such an act, he could not give any reason. Electricity was often utilised in medical treatment around this time, by applying currents to nerve points via a battery and cables. It was believed that the 'life-giving force' of electricity could cure many illnesses and bring people back to life when all signs of life had gone.

6 APRIL

1814   In the Police Court, a carter was fined half a guinea for having forcibly boarded one of the city omnibuses, and assaulted the boy who was on duty as a guard. The omnibus had been on its way to the stable yard after the days' work when, on passing along Gallowgate, three carters jumped on the step, opened the door, seated themselves inside and tried to get possession of the 'bag'. The boy had called to the driver to stop, at which point the carters made their escape.

7 APRIL   **1845**   A man residing in Stockwell Street, said to have been suffering from 'domestic discomfort', swallowed a quantity of laudanum with the intention of taking his own life. This would have no doubt proved successful if it had not been for the prompt application of a stomach pump. Laudanum was an opium-based painkiller which was widely prescribed by doctors in the Victorian era for ailments ranging from headaches to tuberculosis. It was also popular as a recreational drug, particularly among the working classes, as it was cheaper than gin, but was also the drug of choice for suicide attempts at this time.

8 APRIL   **1844**   The murder of a child was reported in the newspapers on this date. The body of a male child, about three or four weeks old, had been found in a quarry in Hillhead, close by the viaduct across the Kelvin, on the Great Western Road. The body had been entirely covered with soft mud, except for one of the feet, and on examination by Drs Easton and McTear, it was concluded that the child must have been alive when thrust under the mud. It had been reported that on the night before the child was found, a 'decently dressed' female had been seen going into the quarry carrying something bulky.

9 APRIL   **1846**   A warning to parents and guardians appeared in the *Glasgow Herald*, telling of the 'dastardly conduct' which had lately been taking place in the city. A 'heartless set of thieves, male and female' had been going around cutting off the graceful ringlets and plats of hair from children who happened to be out of doors unattended. On three or four occasions, the children had had nearly all of their hair cut off.

10 APRIL   **1826**   Whilst a young man named Robb was driving, two horses and carts loaded with stones, from the quarry into the town, a number of schoolgirls were amusing themselves during the midday interval. One of them, seven-year-old Janet Montgomery, came too near the front horse, fell and was killed on the spot by the wheel passing over her head. It was discovered that the driver, rather than having

the reins of the front horse in his hand, had been walking opposite the second cart when the accident occurred. He was charged with culpable homicide.

11 APRIL

1896 A 'terrible tragedy' was reported in the newspapers. In Pollockshaws, Mrs Ellen Hannah, the wife of an iron turner, murdered her three youngest children, aged between five weeks and three years old, by cutting their throats. Mr Hannah had been at his work when the murders took place. Early in the afternoon, a neighbour met Mrs Hannah on the stairs, who was complaining of a sore head. A short time later, there was a 'tremendous knocking' at the door of the MacDougal's, who lived in the same close. The MacDougalls' son Daniel opened the door and found Mrs Hannah there with a razor, which she asked him to sharpen. However, at that time, Daniel noticed that there was blood on her hand and on her dress, accompanied by marks on her neck, which led him to believe she had tried to cut her throat. The young man took the knife from Mrs Hannah, and his mother helped her onto a chair. Stating she 'could not get the other two', she sat down, whilst neighbours went to the Hannahs' house, suspecting that something terrible must have happened. There they found the bloody scene of the children with their throats cut.

At her trial in Glasgow High Court, Mrs Hannah was described as 'a quiet looking woman of middle age', and a plea of insanity was tendered. Medical evidence was given by Drs Walker and Whish, of Pollockshaws, to the effect that they had been summoned to the scene of the tragedy immediately afterwards and from Mrs Hannah's appearance they came to the conclusion that she was suffering from 'melancholia' and was 'of unsound mind'. Other doctors who had examined her at a later time also stated that in their opinion Mrs Hannah was insane and therefore unable to plead to the charge. In light of this evidence, Lord Kincairney ordered her to be detained at Her Majesty's pleasure.

12 APRIL

1844 A man described as 'a very torn down looking fellow' was charged in the Police Court with attempting to steal from a print shop in Gallowgate. It appeared that the prisoner had been caught half in and half out of the back shop window, the heavy window having fallen upon his body and jamming him there, where he had remained until the owners of the shop discovered him.

13 APRIL   **1846** Thomas Gregory, a journeyman painter who resided in High Street, was sent by his employer to work in an unoccupied dwelling in Eglinton Street. From the time he was sent there until two days later, he had never been seen or heard of. As the door of the house in which he was employed was locked from the inside, the door had to be forced open. As this was done, Gregory, who was said to have been suffering from 'delirium tremens', an altered mental state caused by alcohol withdrawal, rushed over to the window, which was on the third floor, and threw himself out.

14 APRIL   **1846** John Angus, the keeper of a tavern in between Glassford Street and Hutcheson Street, was placed at the police bar charged with 'keeping a disorderly house' and with 'entertaining men and women of notoriously bad fame therein, to the disturbance of the neighbourhood'. After the evidence of several respectable neighbours and the watchman, he was found guilty and fined £10.

15 APRIL   **1848** A lady named Mrs Ferguson, described as showing 'the appearance of having seen better days', was charged with having 'imposed on the parish of Glasgow' by swindling orphans out of money. It appeared that Ferguson had laid a trap to deprive 'two apparently decent and respectable girls' of the money allowed for the keeping of their orphan brother and sister, who resided in the parish of Greenock. She was sentenced to twenty days in prison.

16 APRIL   **1847** Shortly before ten o'clock at night, a 'woman of the town', named Mary Mulholland, who resided with a Mrs McLean in a house in King Street, was brought by one of the watchmen to the police office, apparently in a 'dying state'. It appeared from her own statement that she had taken laudanum, which she had purchased from a shop of a surgeon in King Street. She was attended to by the police surgeon, who applied the stomach pump, but his efforts were in vain. Mary Mulholland died during

A laudanum bottle.

the course of the night. Her suicide was said to have been induced by 'despondency superinduced by the privations and wretchedness commonly connected with the course of life she had pursued'.

17 APRIL

1826   Some men who were working in the vicinity of a farmhouse, gave the owner, a Mr Young, 4lbs of gunpowder in a brown paper bag and asked him to keep it for them until the following day. Mr Young laid it on the mantlepiece above the fire in the kitchen, where it was found by his daughter, who was playing and proceeded to make a small hole in the bag with a stick. The powder fell in a small stream into the ash pit and the girl, alarmed by this, ran to alert her mother and sister. They came running in to try and avert danger, but just as they reached the fireplace the stream of powder was ignited and the bag of gunpowder exploded. The house was 'shaken to the foundation' and a back window was blown out. The blast threw Mrs Young and her daughters back against the door. All three were very badly burned; Mrs Young and her eldest daughter so severely burned that they sadly died a few days later.

18 APRIL **1846** In the Police Court, a young man described as 'a ferocious looking young scoundrel' was sentenced to sixty days' imprisonment for 'striking and otherwise maltreating his aged father and mother'. On leaving the bar in custody of an officer, he turned round to the Bench and exclaimed, 'I'll make them pay sweetly for this when I come out.'

19 APRIL **1847** A man named Gavin Duncan, a cooper residing in Gallowgate, accidentally dropped the lighted candle he was holding, among the straw which formed the bed on which his wife lay. The straw quickly caught fire and Mrs Duncan was severely burned. It was reported that both parties were 'much the worse of liquor' at the time the accident occurred.

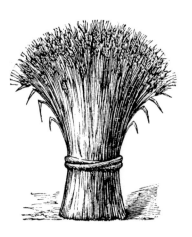

20 APRIL **1846** An article appeared in the *Glasgow Herald* on this date on the subject of 'Unlicensed Penny Theatres':

Unquestionably the numerous penny and half penny unlicensed theatres which, from some cause of other, have been tolerated in Glasgow for so many years, is one of the greatest evils that could be inflicted on the community. There are four places of this description, all near the foot of Saltmarket, where regular stage plays are nightly performed, and sometimes 3 or 4 times a night, and even 5 or 6 times on Saturday nights, to audiences consisting of several thousands of boys and girls, averaging from 5 to 15 years of age; and how these things have been suffered in Glasgow so long is altogether inexplicable to us, for we believe we have the authority of a high public functionary, who for many years has had the best

A close in Saltmarket.

means of watching the progress of crime in this city, for saying – and the records of Bridewell and the House of Refuge prove the fact – that these penny and half penny theatres have been the means of corrupting the morals of thousands of young persons from the neighbouring factories, warehouses, and workshops, who, by the pernicious example of the thieves and prostitutes with whom they are brought into contact in these places, are soon rendered as their associates.

21 APRIL   1826   About one o'clock in the afternoon, a young woman, servant to 'a respectable person in Gallowgate', attempted to drown herself in the Clyde. However, a person passing at the time plunged into the river and managed to prevent her from accomplishing this. The young woman was taken to the Humane Society House in a lifeless state and given medical help.

22 APRIL   1845   At the Police Court, two sisters, named Elizabeth Mitchell and Ellen Mitchell, the former in her twenties and the latter aged nine years old, were placed at the bar accused of stealing 'a number of articles of wearing apparel' from the house in which they had been

lodging. From the evidence it appeared that they had been introduced to the lodgings under the following circumstances: About five weeks before the robbery, the little girl had called at the house which was owned by Mr Thomson and asked for charity. Mr Thomson kindly enquired into the girl's history and she informed him that she was an orphan and that her sister was waiting for her a short distance away. Thinking this was a case of real distress, Mr Thomson allowed both sisters to get their supper, paid for lodgings for the night and told them to come to the house for breakfast the next morning. After this, he got the eldest sister into work and continued to provide them with their breakfast and supper for some time, additionally obtaining respectable lodgings for them. However, in return for all of this kindness shown to them, the girls proceeded to steal a number of articles from Mr Thomson's house. The two sisters were found guilty of the charge and the youngest was sent to the House of Refuge, whilst the eldest was sentenced to sixty days' imprisonment.

23 APRIL

1845 A man named Shields, residing in Main Street, was apprehended and lodged in the Gorbals Police Office for examination, suspected of 'being the cause of his wife's death'. It appeared that Shields had heard of his wife being in a public house in Main Street, drinking with 'some other company'. On going to the public house and finding his wife there, Shields struck her on the side of the head with his fist, after which she left with him to return home. On arriving at their house, Mrs Shields was knocked over and fell on a three legged stool which struck her in the abdomen. Being pregnant at the time, this injury caused her instant death.

24 APRIL

1800 Robert Robertson, accused of the murder or culpable homicide of James Brown, a young boy, was found guilty on this date by his own confession. Robertson stated that he although he caused the boy's death, it had not been his intention to murder him. He was sentenced to banishment from Scotland for life.

25 APRIL

Areas of Glasgow – Govan
Gaining burgh status in 1864, Govan, in the west of Glasgow, became part of the city of Glasgow in 1912. During the eighteenth and nineteenth centuries Govan's industry grew, with textile mills, coal mines and shipbuilding all shaping the district, changing it from a rural area to one of great industrial strength. The population

of Govan increased tenfold during the nineteenth century. This increase led to the inevitable problems of poverty, overcrowding, death and disease faced in other Glasgow areas. Many tenements had no running water or sanitation, providing a breeding ground for diseases such as cholera and typhus. It took until the 1930s, when housing estates were built to help with the overcrowded slum districts, for Govan to recover from the mass immigration of the mid-nineteenth century.

26 APRIL   **1855** A case of 'a ruffian son' was heard in the Eastern District Police Court on this date. A weaver named John McDove was tried and convicted of having 'struck and abused his own father'. It appeared that this had been the twelfth occasion on which he had been brought to the police office for similar offences. Bailie Wright sentenced the 'unfeeling ruffian' to sixty days' imprisonment.

27 APRIL   **1849** A couple of detective officers, on searching a dwelling house in High Street where it was suspected that stolen property had been concealed, were confronted by a young Irish lad who was lodging there. The officers, finding the young lad's attitude impertinent, committed him to custody for disorderly conduct and he was locked up for the night. It was ascertained at the same time that he had in his possession a trunk, which among other things, contained a brace of pistols, and a sum of money amounting to £13. The following morning, an Irishman, stating that he was from County Monaghan, entered the office with a letter from that county in his hand requesting the help of the Glasgow police to assist in finding a young lad who had absconded from his relatives. The lad had taken £15 belonging to his father and a brace of pistols when he left. The boy in custody being identified by the man, the youth was entrusted to his charge and sent back across the channel.

28 APRIL   **1856** The shop of a general dealer in one of the Western Arcades was broken into for the second time in recent months and a number of articles were again stolen. The shop in question was kept by the man's daughter, who on both occasions gave information to the police authorities of the robberies. A variety of circumstances connected with the last robbery, however, awakened the suspicion of Detective Bouker of the Northern District, who instructed officers that the girl's movements should be watched. The next morning, one

of the constables, who was watching in plain clothes, observed her leave a neighbouring shop with a carpet bag. He arrested her and took her to the police office where, on searching the bag, all of the articles reported stolen were found. During the day, a young girl from the south side came to the police office to ask for the prisoner. On leaving, this girl was also followed and a number of the articles stolen from the previous robbery were found in her residence. It was reported that 'bad associates' had induced the girl to steal from her father.

29 APRIL   **1822**   Daniel Rankine, formerly convicted of house breaking, was placed at the bar to receive sentence. Lord Succoth, in pronouncing the sentence of death, told the prisoner to 'act as if his account was closed in this world, and use the little time that was left in preparing for another state'. He was sentenced to be executed on the 5 June.

30 APRIL   **1847**   A young orphan girl about fifteen or sixteen years of age had been brought from a country village to be a nursery maid in a gentleman's family in town. Unfortunately, she had only been in Glasgow around two or three weeks when she became acquainted with Kirsty White, described as a 'char woman or washerwoman', who it was reported, began to corrupt the girl and plied her with whisky. The gentleman, becoming aware of this association, barred the girl from speaking to White again, but she did not heed this warning and continued to visit her. It appeared that White had persuaded the girl to steal several articles from her employer's house, beginning with tea, sugar and soap, progressing to anything she could lay her hands on, such as clothing and silver. The missing articles were found by criminal officers in a pawn shop where White had taken them to be sold. The girl herself, although the thief, was made a witness for the prosecution and Kirsty White was sentenced to twenty days' hard labour in the Bridewell.

MAY

George Square, Glasgow.

1 MAY   **1826** A middle-aged woman, described as 'addicted to drinking' was found dead in her cell in the Bridewell on this date. She had been sentenced to sixty days' imprisonment for the theft of linen shirts and had been confined in the old wing, where she had suspended herself from an iron rod by means of a small cord she had found among the cotton given to her to pick. It appeared that she had eaten her dinner before committing the act and when the female turnkey went to collect the empty dish, the woman had given no indication of her plans.

2 MAY   **1823** A case of grave-robbing was reported in the newspapers on this date. As the watchman had been on duty near the High Church, he had observed a man coming over the wall from the burial ground. Sounding his rattle and summoning assistance, the watchman succeeded in apprehending the man, who had in his possession a sack containing a body. The man was taken to the police office along with the body, which was claimed later by the wife and son of the deceased. The perpetrator had been employed in keeping the shop of a medical person in the town.

3 MAY   **1850** A 'fish hawker' named McDonald, was charged in the Police Court with 'sending or allowing his children to go out and beg'. The case had been reported some weeks ago to the inspector of the poor in the Saltmarket district. Whilst the inspector had been in a shop, two of the children had come in and had been given money by the shop owner to purchase some food, knowing them to be starved at home. The inspector expressed his doubts at the time as to whether

the money would be used for its intended purpose and followed the children, finding as he suspected, that the money was being handed straight over to their father. After only a few minutes, he observed the eldest child being sent out to purchase tobacco with the money they had received. In court, the children were a pitiful sight, dressed in bundles of rags. McDonald was sentenced to sixty days' imprisonment and the children were placed under the charge of the parish.

4 MAY   **1821**   Two men went into a public house in Bridge Street, Tradeston. After drinking some spirits, they got a pack of cards and started to play. They invited the landlord to sit down and drink with them and ordered some wine and took the opportunity whilst the landlord was temporarily distracted, to put a quantity of laudanum into his glass. This he drank and soon after fell asleep, at which point they cut the pocket of his trousers, removed his pocketbook and extracted £60 from it. The landlord still fast asleep, was awakened about three o'clock in the morning by the police watchman, who had entered the house after noticing the door was open.

5 MAY   **1851**   At the Gorbals Police Court, a number of lodging house keepers, mostly from Main Street, Gorbals, were brought before the Bailie on a charge of having their respective promises in 'a filthy and overcrowded condition'. The complaint was raised at the insistence of the Inspector of the Gorbals Parish, as there were a great many cases of fever occurring at the time, believed to be aggravated by the filthy and overcrowded condition of the neighbourhood. The parties brought before the magistrate were all fined.

6 MAY   **1822**   The subject of 'Prison Discipline' was featured in an article in the *Glasgow Herald* on this date:

> Since the days of their cleanliness and salubrity, they have been so managed as to become the great school for crimes and wretchedness; and the public, though beginning to awake, are not yet sufficiently aware of this fact, and sufficiently alarmed at it ... In prisons which are really meant to keep the multitude in order, and to be a terror to evil-doers, there must be no sharing of profits; no visiting of friends; no education but religious education; no freedom of diet; no weavers' looms or carpenters' benches. There must be a great deal of solitude; coarse food; a dress of shame;

A typical nineteenth-
century prison.

hard, incessant, irksome, eternal labour; a planned, and regulated,
and unrelenting exclusion of happiness and comfort.

7 MAY   1821   About seven o'clock in the evening, a five-year-old boy, whilst
playing on the pavement, was severely cut on the face by a young man,
thought to be an army recruit, who deliberately struck him on the face
with the heel of his shoe. A gentleman who was passing, took the man
into custody and he was lodged in the police office, receiving a sentence
of one months confinement in the Bridewell the following morning.

8 MAY   1821   A gentleman residing in James' Court put an end to his
existence in what was described as, 'a fit of mental derangement'.
It was reported that the man had been in a state of despondency for
some days and just before committing the fatal act, had 'broke out in

a frenzy', during which he rifled around the kitchen utensils, and on not finding any suitable implement there, finally took hold of a razor. He was asked by the alarmed residents what he intended to do with the razor, but without replying, he put it to his throat, which he 'severed in a shocking manner' in front of them.

9 MAY

1850　Shortly after midday, a woman leapt into the river near the foot of the South Quay. The plunge in the water and screams for assistance attracted the attention of the policeman on the station, and also of a seaman on board a vessel lying close to the spot. Jumping into the small boat, the seaman succeeded in rescuing the woman before she drowned. On being brought to the police office, she gave her name as Ann Meek, and appeared to be about thirty years old. She stated that she had been 'under the influence of liquor' at the time of the incident. On being placed at the bar of the River Police Court, charged with 'being the worse of liquor, and with wantonly and recklessly throwing herself into the river, to the alarm and annoyance of the lieges and breach of the peace', she turned out to be 'the notorious Miss Meek', who was frequently and heavily fined at the Central Police Court for 'keeping an improper house in Jamaica Street'. She was convicted of the charges and fined two guineas.

10 MAY

1822　Richard Campbell, who was convicted at the Glasgow Circuit Court of having taken part in an attack upon a house in Clyde Street,

The Clyde, where Ann Meek was rescued from drowning.

was whipped through the streets of Glasgow, as per the terms of his sentence. Campbell's crime had been 'mobbing, rioting and entering the house of Mr Provand, Clyde Street' one Sunday afternoon. Having pleaded not guilty, the jury found the charge proven and he was sentenced to fourteen years' transportation in addition to the public flogging. A distinction had been made that Campbell was the ringleader of the mob, and had been the first to force his way into the house, therefore his punishment had been greater than that of the others involved.

About 12 o'clock, a strong detachment of the 4th dragoon guards paraded in front of the jail, and about the same time a party of police and civil officers attended, under the direction of Superintendent Mr Hardie. The prisoner was brought out of the jail by the north door, and bound to a cart which was in waiting. Parties of the dragoons were placed in front and rear to keep the crowd away, and when all were ready, the cavalcade moved round to the area on the south side of the jail where Campbell's back was bared and he was given twenty lashes with the cat-o'-nine-tails. This punishment was then repeated at the foot and head of the Stockwell and last at the Cross, twenty lashes being given each time, making eighty in total. It was reported that he 'appeared to feel the lash very acutely'. When this part of his sentence was completed, he urged the crowd present to take warning by what he had suffered, as from being a spectator, he had been led into taking part in the riot for which he was being punished.

11 MAY   **1844** A young man who gave his name as James Simpson, and who was described as having 'the appearance of a clerk', was charged in the Police Court with disorderly conduct. About ten o'clock on a previous night, the prisoner, accompanied by two females, entered the shop of Dr Tannahill, Sauchiehall Street, for the purpose of making a small purchase. He was 'the worse of liquor' at the time and the boy who had been left in charge of the shop in the absence of the doctor, endeavoured to make Simpson go away. Simpson, however, refused to go and began quarrelling with his companions, who were 'of notoriously bad character'. The girls made an attempt to leave the shop, but Simpson stood between them and the door and would not let them pass. Forcing his way into Dr Tannahill's consulting room, Simpson proceeded to smash several valuable cases of surgical instruments, tore books and papers and overturned the tables and

chairs. Neighbours, on hearing the disturbance, summoned the police, who took him into custody. Simpson was fined £5.

12 MAY

1830   On this date, the public execution of John Hill and William Porter took place. Both had been convicted of assaulting and robbing William Marshall, a seventy-six-year-old man, in Stewart's Road in the north of the city, having struck him 'severe blows on the head'. Marshall had been killed it seems, for his shoes, a pair of spectacles, 7s and a silk handkerchief. At their trial, both men pleaded not guilty, but the jury, after hearing the evidence against them, found them guilty of the crimes. Lord Meadowbank, in passing the death sentence, delivered an address to the prisoners at the bar, which was interrupted by Porter, stating, 'My Lord, have mercy on the panels at the bar.' His Lordship told Porter not to waste his time asking for mercy, as it would be 'utterly in vain'. As they were young men, neither of them above nineteen years old, a number of well-meaning persons had tried to get the sentence commutated, a request which was not granted due to the aggravated nature of the crime. The night before the execution, the parents and friends of the youths were admitted to say their last farewell, with the parting scene between Porter, his mother and sisters described as 'affecting in the highest degree'. The following morning, both prisoners spent time in prayer, before mounting the scaffold. Porter was the one given the handkerchief to signal when they were ready, and in an instant he gave the fatal signal, and the drop fell. They both struggled violently for a few minutes, then the spectacle was over.

13 MAY

1844   At about four o'clock in the morning, the wife of John Mitchell, residing in the Old Vennel, was found dead on the outside staircase at her home. It appeared that she and her husband had both been drinking and had become very intoxicated the previous evening, and that he had gone into the house in 'a state of insensibility', while his wife had remained outside on the stair of the close and died. As no marks of violence were found on her person, death was said to have been entirely the result of the alcohol consumed.

14 MAY

1857   At the Justice of the Peace Court, a thief named James King pleaded guilty to an attempt at housebreaking, and was sentenced to sixty days' imprisonment. It appeared that between the hours of one and three o'clock in the morning, the neighbours of Mrs Campbell, a grocer, were alerted by cries for help. Arriving to assist, they met Mrs Campbell, a widow in her seventies, who had emerged from her dwelling in a state of excitement, declaring that 'there was something in her lum [sic], for there had been an awfu' moaning and the floor was a' covered wi' soot'. The assembled neighbours proceeded to the back of the tenement, when they discovered a ladder propped up against the wall, and a man's coat at the bottom. An ascent was immediately made, when a wail was heard to come from the chimney. On proceeding along the roof, a bar laid across the top of the chimney was discovered, with a rope attached. On looking down the chimney, the head and hand of King were discovered, who had become stuck fast. The rope which the thief had used for his attempted descent was used to pull him up and he eventually emerged, 'as black as soot'.

15 MAY

1826   At the Police Court, James Spence, described as 'a notorious impostor', was placed at the bar. Described as 'a stout, healthy man, rather above fifty years of age', he came forward on this occasion with the stature of a much older man, considerably shaking. Spence had been detected going amongst the gentlemen in Miller Street asking for charity, with a certificate supposedly signed by an elder residing in Anderston, telling a moving tale of distress. As suspected by the gentlemen, this certificate turned out to be a forgery. Bailie Hinshaw on sentencing, commented that 'he was well aware that the public were frequently imposed on by vagrants of this description' and that 'such conduct could not be tolerated at this time of such general distress'. Spence was sent to the Bridewell for thirty days.

16 MAY

1845   As the seven o'clock train from Greenock was leaving the terminus at Bridge Street, a charman, named Robert Andrew boarded one of the carriages and continued standing for a short distance, when he suddenly jumped down, and in doing so fell with one of his legs upon the rail. The train ran over his leg, which was instantly severed from his body.

17 MAY

1850   A report was received at the Southern Police Office that a woman had that morning, met with a severe accident from burning, in Main Street, Gorbals. The woman, it seems, had been attending a family who had been ill with fever, the father having died from the same fever the previous day in the Royal Infirmary. Whilst getting up during the night to give one of the children a drink, she passed too

Bridge Street
railway station.

near to the fire, and with her nightdress catching fire, she was soon
enveloped in flames. Another woman, who came to her assistance,
also ended up having her hands, arms and other parts of her body
dreadfully burned.

18 MAY   1821   A four-year-old child, the son of Alexander Bayn, miller at
the Dean Mill, had been permitted to go to the mill after lunch to
play. Later that afternoon, it was discovered that the boy had gone
missing, and after an extensive search had been carried out, he was
still nowhere to be found. The next day, however, it was discovered
that he had fallen into the mill-lead, and that by the suction of the
water he had been drawn into an iron tunnel that served the great
wheel. The grim discovery had been made by a young sweep-boy who
found the body when he entered the tunnel.

19 MAY   1820   A private of the Rifle Brigade, named Henderson ended up
with the top of one of his thumbs hacked off on this date. It appeared,
however, that Henderson himself had been the person who hacked
the part off. Whilst sitting on one of the seats on the green, he made
at least two cuts with the hatchet; the first going through the nail
of the thumb, and the second further up. The parts were afterwards
found by two of the county patrol near the seat, and the hatchet
secreted under some turf. As this was a transportable offence, he was
reported to the authorities.

20 MAY

1820 About six o'clock, as a man employed at one of the cotton mills in Bridgetown was entering the green on his way home, two strangers came behind and fired at him with pistols. The pistols were loaded with swan shot and one bullet went through his thigh, whilst another was lodged in his shoulder. Another of the workers passing a short time later was also fired at; however, spotting the pistol just in time, he ducked and the shot went over him.

21 MAY

1855 Whilst a gentleman was in his house in West Regent Street, he became aware of an escape of gas in the lobby of his dwelling house. Fortunately, he soon found someone to repair the leak, and in the afternoon it was assumed that all was well again. The next morning, however, he once again noticed an odour of gas, and, with the aid of a pair of ladders, he ascended with a lighted paper to examine the lustre, which was attached to a broad ornamental arch that stretched across the ceiling. Lighting a small blue flame at the root of the pipe, he instantly observed the plaster move. Realising the danger, he slid down the steps to the floor; however, before he could reach the ground an explosion which shook the whole tenement. On emerging from the cloud of dust and broken plaster, he discovered that the arch was completely blown to pieces and the lustre with all its chains and pipes, lay smashed on the floor. Fifteen panes of glass above the front door were also blown, and, consequently, a mass of debris law across the street. It was discovered that the repair man, in fixing the original problem, had accidentally broken part of the plaster, which allowed the gas to escape.

22 MAY

1851 A young man named Michael Prior was placed at the bar of the Calton Police Court, charged with having two days previously, cut about a pound of hair from the tails of a number of cattle which were standing in a byre in the Cattle Market. Prior had regularly been in the vicinity of the Cattle Market, but had managed to commit this type of theft for a considerable time without detection. Mr Colquhoun, the tracksman of the Cattle Market, and had even asked Prior to keep a look out for anyone committing such an act, not realising that Prior was in fact the plunderer.

23 MAY

1851 With fever being widespread in the city at this time, the following comments were featured in the *Glasgow Herald*:

Of late, the police authorities have been exceedingly active in their exertions for the suppression of low lodging houses, and really the exposure which has been made of the crowds of wretched beings of both sexes huddled up in miserable dens, the very nurseries of disease, immorality and crime, can only impress one with the feeling that it is a wonder mortality is not greater amongst us than it has been.

24 MAY   **1851** At the Eastern District Court, John Riddell was brought before the sitting magistrate on a 'rather serious charge of assault' upon a police constable. From the evidence it appeared that the defendant, who was 'much the worse of drink', had insulted the

Left and above: Inside a typical Victorian low lodging house.

night watchman on London Road. The constable took the man into custody and endeavoured to take him to the police office, but on the way he resisted violently, striking the watchman on the face, and hacking at his uniform with a shoemaker's knife cut. Riddell was fined three guineas.

25 MAY   1852   On this date, a man named David Gilmour was found dead in his house in Kelvin Street. It appeared that Gilmour, who was a mason, and a fairly young man, had 'abandoned himself to the wildest debauchery' since the death of his mother six weeks before. He had been continually drinking with a number of persons who were said to have 'preyed upon him till the whole of his spare clothes and all the furniture his house contained had disappeared'. When the house was entered, he was found lying dead among the rubbish of the fireplace. It was assumed that he must have risen during the night to take a drink of water and had fallen down and perished in the attempt.

26 MAY   1856   During the morning, a violent explosion occurred at the house of a widow named Mrs Beglie in McAlpine Street. She had thrown a pair of old shoes on the kitchen fire for the purpose of burning them, when within a few minutes, there was an explosion, which blew out the wall that divided the kitchen from the closet. It was supposed that some gun powder had been concealed in one or other of the shoes. Mrs Beglie's son was questioned, but denied knowing anything about the powder.

27 MAY   1855   A nine-year-old child named John Aitken was found 'in a state of wretched destitution', begging upon the public streets within the boundary of the City Parish. He was taken to the Town's Hospital, where he was washed, clothed and fed, prior to being placed at the bar of the Police Court and convicted under the Reformatory Schools Act. His mother, described as 'a worthless person', appeared along with him. It was discovered that she had four other children, all working for their own maintenance and living separately from her, and that she had been in the habit of sending the little boy out to beg. The boy was sent to a Reformatory School for five years.

28 MAY   1827   Two young girls were caught in the act of attempting to strip a little boy of his clothes in a close in Nelson Street. They managed to

escape however, and immediately went to the other side of the Clyde, where they stripped two other children completely. They were pursued by some boys and eventually taken into custody. It was reported that they were both sisters, and their mother was 'a notorious resetter' and an inmate of the Bridewell. Reset was the crime of 'feloniously receiving or retaining goods, obtained by theft, robbery [...], knowing that they have been dishonestly appropriated'.

29 MAY   **1821**   On this date, the sad discovery was made of the body of a newborn child among the rubbish, opposite the washing house in the Green. There was a high rate of child mortality at this time and cases of 'infanticide' were common. This was due to a lack of reliable contraception, conditions being over crowded, together with there being no legal or even safe abortion facilities for the poor.

30 MAY   **1851**   Two little girls, aged seven and ten years old respectively, were found in a close in Main Street in a state of nudity. It appeared that they had been in the Town's Hospital and their father, described as being 'of dissipated habits', had called and requested to get them out, claiming that he was in a position to provide for them. However, on getting the girls out, he took them into the close and stripped them of all their clothes, which he pawned to get money for drink.

31 MAY   **1852**   An elderly female, named Mrs McNamara, residing in the Gorbals, was engaged in helping some neighbours to move house. Whilst doing so, she saw what seemed to be a bottle of whisky in their house, and without asking put it to her lips and took a gulp. Unfortunately for Mrs McNamara though, the liquid she had swallowed turned out to be a preparation used by tinsmiths for lackering, which was a well-known active poison.

JUNE

Great Western Road, 1900.

1 JUNE

1876 Thomas Barr, who had been convicted at the Glasgow Circuit Court of the murder of his wife and mother in law, was executed in the South Prison. Barr had married his wife Margaret in 1874, and at the time he, being some fourteen years older than her, had four children from a previous marriage. A year after their marriage, Margaret gave birth to a son, who sadly died the same day. After this point, Barr seemed to have taken on the notion that his wife had been unfaithful to him, although there was no reason for him to have come to this conclusion. As a result, he became very unkind to Margaret and her mother, often threatening his wife with a poker or a knife if she tried to leave him. However, managing to get away from him, Margaret had gone to her mother's house in Gallowgate, only for Barr to turn up there on that fateful day with a knife. Forcing his way into the house, he stabbed his mother-in-law, then his wife who had come to her assistance. The older woman died instantly, but Margaret was taken to the Royal Infirmary with her serious injuries, dying eventually from a 'large collection of blood in her chest'.

As was often the case, Barr spent the days leading up to his execution in prayer. Just before eight o'clock in the morning, the procession from the condemned cell was heard slowly proceeding along the lobby and the magistrates formally handed Barr over to the executioner, who led him to the scaffold. He was placed on the drop and a belt fastened under his knees, all the while continuing to pray. The white cap was then placed over his head and the drop fell. It was reported that the body twitched for about a minute, but death had been 'almost instantaneous'.

2 JUNE

1924 A terrible tragedy was reported in the newspapers, which had taken place in the one-bedroom apartment in Springfield Place, near Garscube Road. Charles Boyle, aged twenty-seven, who had been an inmate of Stobhill Hospital, had come from the institution in the evening to visit his mother, with whom he was 'not on the best of terms'. Late in the evening, neighbours had heard quarrelling in the Boyles' house, but had paid little attention to it at the time. However,

Buchanan Street.

after one of the neighbours heard a sound which she thought was someone moaning, Sarah Boyle, the youngest of Mrs Boyle's children, got a key and opened the door. She was heard a few minutes later screaming on the landing. Sarah Boyle, on entering the house, found her mother and two young children, who were the son and daughter of neighbour William Devlin, lying in a pool of blood on the floor with their throats cut. A short time after the alarm was raised, detectives arrived on the scene. Upon their arrival, they found Mrs Boyle's body lying in front of the bed, the bodies of young William Devlin at the fireside, and little May Devlin near the doorway.

The two murdered children had been out playing in the back court and had entered the close to shelter when the rain came on, before going into Mrs Boyle's house. Steps were taken to trace Charles Boyle, described as 'a cripple'. However at about midnight, Boyle walked into the police office where he was informed by the officer on duty that he was wanted for the murder of his mother and two children. He was reported to have replied 'I did it', and was immediately placed under arrest. Shortly before the incident, Boyle's movements had not been out of the ordinary. He had been seen entering a close in Garscube Road where two young men were playing cards, and after watching the game for a short time, he was given 3½ *d* from them to buy fish and chips, after which he proceeded to his mother's house.

3 JUNE

1893 Susan Maitland attempted to hold her three-year-old son John over a boiler of pitch in Buchanan Street, in the hope that the fumes would cure him of whooping cough. As she was having difficulty holding the child herself, a man named Patrick McMahon stepped in to help. McMahon, however, ended up losing his balance, and he and the child both fell into the boiling pitch.

4 JUNE

1847 One of the workmen in Mr Biggart's woollen factory in Dalry met with a fatal accident. The workman, Michael Findlay, had been putting a belt on a drum when he was caught by the hand and carried round the shaft several times before anyone saw what was happening. Several local doctors arrived on the scene and did everything in their power to help. Findlay survived for thirty-six hours after the accident, but in the end his injuries proved too great.

5 JUNE

1846 At three o'clock in the morning in King Street, Tradeston, a woman named Kerr, who had been sitting too close to a lighted

Buchanan Street: an alternative street scene.

candle in her house, was burned to death. The deceased, who was heavily pregnant, was said to have been 'literally scorched to a cinder'. Inquiries found that both she and her husband were both intoxicated when the horrific accident occurred.

6 JUNE   **1851**   At around half past five o'clock in the morning, the body of a woman, appearing to be about twenty-two years old, was observed floating in the river opposite Nelson's monument. Mr Geddes, keeper of the Humane Society's house, on hearing of this, immediately proceeded to the spot and had the body brought ashore. It was thought that the body had not been in the water long, with the fatal occurrence probably taking place the previous night.

7 JUNE   **1849**   A matter of 'Caution to Master Chimney Sweepers' was reported in the newspapers. At the Police Court, Messrs McLean, Campbell & Wilson were charged with employing young boys to clean chimneys and flues. This was the first case of its kind to be

A scene from the *Illustrated Police News*, © The British Library.

STABBED OVER A GAME OF CARDS.

tried in Scotland since the passing of the Act for the regulation of Chimney Sweepers and Chimneys, as since 1842 it had been illegal to use children to ascend or descend chimneys or enter flues, due to the cruelty of this practice. The parties admitted the charged and were fined £5 each, the magistrate remarking that 'those who knowingly permitted young boys to ascend of descend chimneys or flues in their premises' were equally to blame.

8 JUNE

1925   In the Sheriff Court, James Leyden was convicted of having assaulted his wife and fifteen-month-old child, by kicking and striking them with his fists, in their house in Portland Street, severely injuring the child. Leyden was sentenced to four months' imprisonment with hard labour.

9 JUNE

1900   A card game played by two Italian men in a shop in Main Street, Gorbals ended in a quarrel. As one of them, Carlo Giuliani, rose to leave, the other, Carlo Ostini, stabbed him so severely that he died within a few minutes. There were a number of eye witnesses to the murder, which was over a dispute about money. It was reported that Ostini was 'much indebted' to wholesale wine and provisions merchant, Giuliani, and on the day of the incident had been seeking another advance of money, which Giuliani refused. Ostini, angry at this refusal, drew a dagger from his pocket and plunged it into the chest of Giuliani, who dropped on his knees from the force of the blow. Having swiftly withdrawn the dagger, Ostini was about to plunge it into Giuliani's chest a second time, when two other men, Ralph Categnani and Ugo Andrucci, rushed at him and seized him by the arms. By the time the police and the local doctor arrived, Giuliani was dead. At Ostini's trial it was deemed that a verdict of guilty to culpable homicide was appropriate, as it was accepted that Ostini had lost his temper in the heat of the moment and had not set out to kill Giuliani. He was sentenced to ten years' penal servitude.

10 JUNE

1850   The steamer *Orion* was on her passage to Greenock, ending in a far more dramatic fashion than most of her journeys. Onboard the vessel a young man in the steerage, who was travelling to Glasgow, pulled a razor from his pocket, and in the presence of a large number of other passengers, cut his throat from ear to ear. Despite every assistance being rendered, the young man died shortly afterwards. No motive was found for his putting an end to his life in this way.

11 JUNE   **1848**   At Anderson Police Court, three young boys were charged with stealing a quantity of clothes from a bleaching green at Sauchiehall Street. One of the boys, who was not more than five years old, had crept through a small gap in a wall or hedge, and hauled out the clothes to his older associates, who then ran off with the items. The boys were pursued and apprehended soon afterwards. The two eldest boys were each sentenced to imprisonment for thirty days; but the other, due to his age, was sent to the Industrial School.

12 JUNE   **1897**   The execution of George Paterson of Pollockshaws was reported in the newspapers on this date. On the morning in question, at eight o'clock, he suffered 'the extreme penalty of the law' in Glasgow Gaol for the murder of his lover. There had been an effort made to obtain a commutation of the death sentence, but the Secretary for Scotland could see no ground for interference, and so George Paterson saw out his sentence on the scaffold. When informed a few days earlier that his life would not be spared, Paterson had become resigned to his fate and engaged in prayer with the prison chaplain. The murder had been carried out in Paterson's home in Milton Lane, Glasgow, where he had assaulted Ann McGuire, who lived with him, with a red hot poker. As Ann was dying she told police that Paterson had made the poker red hot in the fire and had struck her all over her body with it, angry that she had taken money out of his pocket to pay the rent.

13 JUNE   **1848**   James Smith, a deaf and dumb man residing in New Street, Calton, committed a 'savage and unprovoked assault' upon a woman named Susan MacDonald. Under the influence of alcohol, Smith struck and kicked the woman so severely, she was lucky to escape with her life. Neighbours hearing the commotion were said to have intervened just in time. He was sentenced to sixty days' imprisonment.

14 JUNE   **1890**   A fire broke out in the dwelling house of Joseph Evans, a labourer, in Richard Street on this date. The fire was fairly small and easily containable. However, Mrs Evans, who was home with her two children, having taken fright and becoming confused by the smoke, rushed to a window of the fourth-storey dwelling and jumped out. Mrs Evans sustained such horrific injuries in the fall that she did not survive through the night. The fire brigade, having arrived speedily, managed to put out the flames, but unfortunately on searching the

rooms the found the sad remains of the two children, who had been left behind.

15 JUNE   **1934**   A young woman appeared on an unusual charge at Glasgow Sheriff Court. The accused pleaded guilty to having a smoothing iron on the window sill of a house in Lawmoor Street without sufficiently guarding the iron from being blown or thrown down. The result of this was that it fell and struck eight-year- old James Jackson, causing him an injury to his head which resulted in temporary paralysis and required hospital treatment.

16 JUNE   **1897**   Samuel Gillon, described as 'a wretched looking man', was charged with having assaulted his wife by cutting her on the cheek and neck with a razor, at their house in Green Street, Calton. Mrs Gillon stated that she and her husband had been married for thirty-eight years, and worked together in a tobacco factory. On the night in question, she and her husband 'had a little drink', and when they returned to the house, her husband got into a quarrel with a neighbour. Mrs Gillon tried to patch up the disagreement, but her husband took exception to this and taking out a razor, proceeded to attack her with it. The jury, without leaving the box, brought in a verdict of guilty. Gillon was sentenced to eighteen months' imprisonment.

17 JUNE   **1926**   Police Constable George Massie appeared before the Stipendiary Magistrate at the Central Police Court, charged with assaults on five men and two women. Evidence was given by several witnesses who stated that the accused, whilst in the Southside, had proceeded to go around launching unprovoked attacks on people in the vicinity, striking them and pushing them to the ground. He was sentenced to thirty days' imprisonment.

18 JUNE   **1939**   In another case of assault, George Thomson admitted at the Southern Police Court, a charge of assaulting his wife and a man. The Fiscal described the case as 'the most diabolical of its kind it had been his lot to hear'. At about half past ten o'clock on a previous night, the accused's wife had met him in Nelson Street. Seeing that he was much under the influence of drink, she took him home and to pacify him, she then went out for cigarettes. On her return, Thomson struck her a brutal blow on the face, at which point she

Glasgow Bridge.

ran out to summon the police. When Mrs Thomson returned with the police, she found her uncle, John Smith, lying unconscious and unrecognisable on the floor. Thomson was sent to prison for thirty days.

19 JUNE

1826 At around 12 o'clock in the morning, while a poor man was going along the Old Bridge, he was attacked, knocked down, severely injured and robbed. On giving the alarm, his attacker ran off, but was pursued by a police watchman who, after a lengthy chase, apprehended the man in Stockwell Street.

20 JUNE

1860 At between two and three o'clock in the morning, a cotton spinner named Alex Seaton, took his own life by hanging. Seaton was found by a slater named David Henderson, suspended by the neck by his own cravat, which was attached to a paling in the close of his Havannah Street home. Seaton had twisted the cravat round his neck and then tied the ends to the paling, suspending himself a few feet from the ground. It was reported that he had been 'dissolute in his habits for some time past, and had in consequence not been on agreeable terms with his wife'.

21 JUNE

1847 A soldier of the rank lance corporal, was convicted in the Police Court of having 'cut through the ear of a poor girl of the town'. The assault had occurred at four o'clock in the morning on the same day, in the New Wynd. The court, who were said to be horrified at the barbarity of the action, sentenced the soldier to thirty days' imprisonment.

22 JUNE

1849 As a labourer named Patrick Hughes was passing Adelphi Street, on the south side of the river, he observed a carter lying on the ground at the end of Stockwell Bridge, sound asleep from the effects of too much alcohol. Looking around him and seeing that no one was near, Hughes proceeded to rifle the pockets of the unconscious carter, from whom he stole 6s and 4¼d. He was in the process of making off the money, when he was apprehended by one of he night watchmen who had observed the whole act. Hughes was sentenced to thirty days' imprisonment.

23 JUNE

1853 At the Central Police Court, John Devlin, a broker in Princes Street, was summoned to answer to an assault committed upon a woman in his own premises. It appeared from the statement of the principal witness, that on the day in question she had called to redeem certain articles which had been pledged some time before for a sum far below their value. However, Devlin coolly told her that he had never done business with her. Surprised at this assertion, the woman remonstrated with him, to which Devlin responded by striking her on the cheek. The charged was found proven and he was fined two guineas, with Bailie Gilmour condemning 'the incivility and rudeness with which poor people were frequently treated by some pawnbrokers.'

24 JUNE

1853 Also at the Central Police Court, a young man, named Currie, who was well known in petty crime circles, was charged with breaking a looking glass and with an assault on a man who made his living in Jail Square by 'amusing the lieges by arrow shooting'. Hugh Smith, who resided in a caravan, from outside of which he sold soda, had placed a large mirror at the side in order to see anyone attempting to commit theft when his back was turned to the crowd. Having learned in the morning that a gang of thieves had planned to break this mirror, a watch had been set up to apprehend the culprits. Currie, having been caught in the act of lifting a stone and throwing it, was found guilty by the court and sentenced to sixty days' imprisonment with hard labour.

25 JUNE

1847 A report appeared in the newspapers on this date of an alleged murder in Main Street, Calton. It appeared that a woman named Agnes Sutherland, residing at 14 Main Street, described as being 'of intemperate habits', had been cohabiting with a sheriff officer named Smith, and on the morning in question, about quarter past three o'clock, the neighbours were alarmed by cries of 'murder' from the woman. At about four o'clock, Smith was seen to leave the house, when a neighbour, alarmed at the earlier sound of a heavy fall, entered the house and found Agnes Sutherland dead on the floor. Smith was apprehended, but a post-mortem found no marks of violence on Agnes' body and Smith was subsequently freed from prison. It was thought that she died from '*delirium tremens*'.

26 JUNE

1853 John Campbell, well known to the detective force as 'an incorrigible thief', was brought up at the Central Police Court charged with assaulting Mrs Gray, a woman residing in New Vennel. Mrs Gray, it seems, had been a very important witness in a case of murder. Whilst buying some fish, she had been accosted by the prisoner, who seized her by the wrist and led her across the street to a quiet corner. When Mrs Gray's husband intervened, Campbell told him that he would 'give him as much as had been given to the murdered man'. Campbell denied the charges against him. However Bailie Gilmour stated that 'there was not a vestige of doubt as to the guilt of the prisoner', additionally commenting that 'if witnesses for the Crown were to be intimidated, the law might be evaded, and the ends of justice completely frustrated'. Campbell was sentenced to sixty days' imprisonment with hard labour.

27 JUNE

1940 A middle-aged man named Daniel Craig appeared in court for stealing a number of articles from a tenement house and then setting it on fire. It was reported that Craig's home was situated in the same tenement building as the one he had set fire to and that his wife and child were asleep at home at the time. Craig's advocate advised the court that two years previously, Craig had been assaulted in the streets of Glasgow and sustained severe head injuries and although he had been found by the doctor to be sane, apparently he had never been quite the same since the attack. Taking this into account, his Lordship sentenced Craig to a reduced sentence of six months 'imprisonment.

28 JUNE

Glasgow Institutions – Glasgow Lunatic Asylum

1804 saw the formation of the Committee of Management of the Glasgow Lunatic Asylum, followed in 1810 by the commencement of the construction of the asylum premises. By 1814 the building was up and running, with inmates segregated by gender and by social class. A report on the institution in 1820, gives an insight into the bizarre treatments carried out at a time when very little was known about the nature of mental illness:

> The treatment of the patients has been varied, according to the features and the cause of their lunacy. Internal remedies have, in a few instances, been of great service, but in general, medicine has been of little avail. The warm bath, sometimes conjoined with the effusion of cold water on the patient's shaven head, has been much used, and often with advantage. Some patients have derived benefit from the cold bath. Exercise, especially in the open air, has been of general utility; and much good has been done, in several cases, by pretty severe bodily labour. Rotary motion, by means of a whirling chair, has of late been tried in a great number of cases, and in some of them, with wonderfully good effects.

In 1843 the asylum moved to new premises at Gartnavel, with extensions to this building added at the end of the nineteenth century and early twentieth century. The number of 'pauper lunatics' had began to decline from the end of the nineteenth century, however, due to the introduction of parochial asylums, although a significant number of paying patients were still treated there. The asylum was renamed the Glasgow Royal Mental Hospital in 1931.

29 JUNE

1820 The case of 'an alarming affray' which occurred in the Saltmarket, was reported on this date. Between seven and eight o'clock in the evening, whilst a dozen soldiers were walking up the

Saltmarket, they were verbally abused by a group of 'blackguard young fellows'. Responding to this, the soldiers drew their bayonets and soon afterwards the police arrived. By this time a crowd had formed and all parties had progressed to the Trongate, where a riot broke out. The soldiers, who no one had dared approach due to their bayonets, were eventually overpowered and taken to the police office. Many of the soldiers, police and local people were injured in the disturbance, some seriously.

30 JUNE

1937 A blind man appeared before the magistrate at Glasgow Northern Police Court on a charge of murdering his ten-year-old stepdaughter and the attempted murder of his blind and deaf wife. The accused, forty-two-year-old Alexander McMillan, was said to have cut a gas pipe in their house in Wigton Street and allowed the gas to escape in the house. Described as 'a well built man with greying hair', McMillan had been detained following the discovery of his wife and stepdaughter suffering from gas poisoning.

JULY

Glasgow trams in operation, *c.* 1910.

1 JULY

1857 Peter Kelly, a labourer from Armour Street, appeared in the Sheriff Court on a charge of having assaulted his wife and causing her death. Kelly was committed to prison for further examination and a post-mortem was ordered. Kelly had been a returned convict, having been sentenced to seven years' transportation for a housebreaking offence five years before. After serving three years of this sentence he had been liberated with a ticket of leave and had been working in Wales, where he had met his wife, before returning to live in Glasgow. Kelly and his wife, who had been on good terms whilst in Wales, had begun to quarrel frequently in Glasgow due to having money problems there.

On the night of the incident, Kelly's mother, who lived with the couple, had gone out to the well and on her return found Mrs Kelly lying on her back on the floor with her head resting on a large iron pot and her infant child beside her. Mrs Kelly had been bleeding profusely from the mouth and nose. Peter Kelly who was sitting on a stool nearby, denied all knowledge of what had happened to his wife, but ran off when neighbours went to summon the police. He was later apprehended in the Gallowgate with blood stains apparent on his clothing. On examination by the doctor, Mrs Kelly was thought to have died from multiple blows to the head. A hammer lying nearby was thought to be the murder weapon. However, following the post-mortem, Kelly was liberated from custody due to the findings indicating that the injuries sustained by Mrs Kelly had not been the cause of her death.

2 JULY

1924 The murder trial of Charles Boyle came to an end. Boyle had been arrested in June of the same year for the murder of his mother and the two young children of a neighbour, in his mother's house at Springfield Place. The trial had been proceeding since the beginning of the week, but it was brought to an abrupt end following the tendering of a plea of culpable homicide by the accused, which was accepted. The sentence handed down to Boyle was fifteen years' penal servitude. Boyle, an inmate of Stobhill Hospital, had gone to his mother's house and cut her throat and the throats of the two children the previous month (See 2 June).

It had been proved in court that it was the accused and no other who had killed Mrs Boyle and the two children; however, the defence had failed to substantiate their special defence of insanity which they had tendered. There were, however, facts which had been proved which pointed towards the fact that although Boyle was sane, he had been suffering from 'certain aberrations of mind or mental unsoundness', and therefore not fully responsible for the actions which he had committed. Lord Ormidale, in passing sentence, said that in his judgement, 'the case involved a great deal of culpability and one could not but feel that when the accused commenced his trial he was in grave jeopardy of his own life.' It was established that Boyle had been intoxicated on the evening in question; however, the court took the view that 'intoxication was no excuse whatever, and it in no way warranted the court from regarding the crime as a most atrocious and highly unjustifiable one'. In court, Boyle was described as 'a very dangerous criminal' and it was highlighted that he had previously been 'mentally defective' and an inmate of Stoneyetts Mental Institution, from which he had escaped. He had been no stranger to appearing in court, having been 'a man of violent passion and temper'.

3 JULY

1820   In the Sheriff Court, Henry Farrel and Robert McLardy, who were described as being 'habit and repute thieves' were accused of theft. Being found guilty, the two men were sentenced to be whipped in the two courts of the jail on Wednesday 12 July, receiving forty stripes in each court. They also received the sentence of banishment from the county for ten years.

4 JULY

1847   A thirteen-year-old boy, described as 'a fine boy', fell in the canal whilst fishing and was drowned. He had been with some friends who gave the alarm, but unfortunately two men who were working nearby, although hearing the cries, misunderstood the meaning of them. Prior to this incident, it had been the practice of boys of similar age to cry out when a fish had been caught.

5 JULY

1822   A woman described as 'stout and fresh looking', seized the opportunity whilst several gentlemen were looking in her direction, to throw herself down on the ground as if having a fit, appearing to be in great distress and vomiting blood. The gentlemen as expected, ran to her assistance, and once recovered, she told them that she was needing to return to her home town of Perth. On receiving the money for her fare, she went on her way, only to repeat the act in front of some other men. Unfortunately for her, however, one of these men had seen her earlier performance, and on challenging the woman, it

Hazardous waters of Glasgow: the scene of many a drowning.

was found that her fits were feigned and that the supposed blood was chewed up chips of Brazil wood.

6 JULY

1858 A tobacco pipe maker named Kelman, living near the High Street, was apprehended along with his wife, on a charge of deserting their children and not providing them with sufficient food and clothing. It appeared that Kelman and his wife left their home for 'a drinking bout', and when they did not return two days later, their neighbours, knowing that there were four young children in the house, became concerned and sent for the police. The four children, aged between nine weeks and six years old, were taken to the police office to be cared for. They had been found in 'a most pitiable, emaciated condition', huddled together in a corner amongst some straw, cold and hungry. Taking the parents into custody, the authorities sent the children to the Town's Hospital.

7 JULY

1848 A woman named Coraghan, residing in Finnieston, was apprehended on a charge of culpable homicide. Four weeks previously, a young boy had been struck on the chest with the handle of a short broom by the woman whilst she was sweeping out a close. Almost immediately after receiving the injury, the boy became unwell and although medical assistance had been obtained for him, he died two weeks later, at which point the sequence of events was reported to the police.

8 JULY

1925   At about five o'clock in the afternoon, a woman named Elizabeth Brown, who was working at the Clydebank Printfield, west of Anderston, accidentally got her hair caught by the 'wash wheel'. Before help could get to her, the wheel lifted her up and she was severely injured, with her right arm being almost severed from her body. Elizabeth Brown was immediately taken to the Royal Infirmary, where the arm had to be amputated.

9 JULY

1847   During the afternoon, a confectioner, who had been in 'rather a desponding state of mind for sometime back, though not so much so as to occasion alarm to his relatives', committed suicide whilst his wife had been out of the house for only a few minutes. On returning home, she had been horror-struck at finding her husband suspended by some yarn with a noose made in it, attached to the wall with a large nail.

10 JULY

1862   A report of a 'murder of almost unexampled ferocity' was reported in the newspapers. The murder was perpetrated in the west end of the city, under mysterious circumstances, and, at this time, no motive had been ascertained for the act. The victim, Jessie MacPherson, was in her thirties and employed as a domestic servant by John Fleming, an accountant. Fleming's house was a two-storey building with a basement flat, the occupants of which were his family, consisting of his son and father. On the previous Friday afternoon, Mr Fleming and his son had proceeded, as they often did, to their other house at Dunoon, leaving his eighty-seven-year-old father, James Fleming, in the house with Jessie MacPherson. According to James Fleming, at around four o'clock

Glasgow Royal Infirmary buildings today.

on the Saturday morning, he was awoken by two or three screams coming from the lower part of the house, but thinking that Jessie may have brought a female friend in to stay with her and this noise may be due screams of laughter, he paid no attention to it. Later that day, seeing Jessie's bedroom door closed, Mr Fleming said that he had assumed that she had gone out, and by Monday, when his son and grandson returned, he still had not seen Jessie, and was still under the assumption that she had left the house. However, suspecting that all was not well, John Fleming went to the basement flat to investigate.

He found the door locked and the key missing, but using the pantry key he was able to gain access. There he found the body of Jessie MacPherson lying on the floor, face down and in a state of nudity. The matter was reported to the police straight away, who determined that she had been hit on the head with a heavy and sharp instrument and her jaw had been smashed. Jessie's clothes were strewn about the room, covered with blood, and her bed sheet, also bloodstained, was found wrapped up and placed behind the door. Streaks of blood were also found leading from this room to the kitchen, and it was established that the murder must have been committed in the kitchen and the body dragged into the bedroom. The police, however, were unable to ascertain how the murderer could have possibly entered or left the house. The original assumption that the motive was robbery, was given credibility by the discovery that some articles of silver were missing from the house. Information later came forward from a previous servant named Mrs McLachlan, however, which indicated that James Fleming was in the habit of treating Jessie to a drink in the kitchen, whilst the family were absent. It emerged that he had also asked Jessie to marry him on several occasions, which she had always refused. Another witness, who often went round the houses doing jobs such as washing stairs for money, had been to the house on the Saturday morning, and reported that James Fleming had asked her to clean part of the lobby. For this task, he brought her the bucket of water and a cloth and would not allow her to go downstairs to empty the water afterwards. The evidence seemed very incriminating against James Fleming, who was taken into custody; however, suspicion soon fell on Mrs McLachlan. It emerged that she and her husband had been involved in the theft of the silver from the house, a discovery which came to light as they tried to pawn a silver plate.

Later evidence also emerged when Mrs McLachlan's blood-soaked clothing was found dumped in a field. Jessie McLachlan was found guilty and sentenced to death.

11 JULY   **1855**   In the evening at about nine o'clock, a servant girl was among the audience of 'Batty's Menagerie'. Whilst watching the keeper putting the lion through his performance, she came too close to the den of the leopard, which swiped at her face – lacerating it severely with one of its claws.

12 JULY   **1850**   A dreadful incident described as 'a distressing example of the result of intoxication', occurred at the house of a marble cutter named Stevenson, in North Woodside Road. His wife, who, two weeks previously, had given birth to a female child, went to sleep in the evening in a state of intoxication, with the infant in her arms. On waking up in the morning, it was found that the child was dead, having been smothered during the night.

13 JULY   **1845**   A boy of about fourteen years of age was taken out of one of the penny theatrical booths at the foot of the Saltmarket, in a state of intoxication. He had been disturbing the house by yelling and striking anyone within his reach. The police were called and carried the drunken boy to the courthouse opposite the Green. There he became more infuriated, breaking six panes of glass and attempting to break more. He was sentenced to sixty days' imprisonment.

14 JULY

1898 A murder described as 'one of the most shocking murders which has occurred in Glasgow for many years' was reported in the newspapers. The victim was Christina Taylor, a fifty-seven-year-old mill worker living in Pleasance Street, Pollockshaws. However, the incident took place, in a one-roomed house occupied by her son, Robert McFarlane, at Reid Street, Bridgeton. John Bryson, a hammerman employed at the shipbuilding yard, and his wife, were lodging with Robert, having returned to Glasgow from America. On the Saturday afternoon, Mrs Taylor had come over to the house and met the Brysons there. The Brysons had been drinking and when Mrs Taylor arrived, Mrs Bryson left to go and buy more whisky, leaving John Bryson and Mrs Taylor alone in the house.

When Robert McFarlane's daughter arrived about an hour later, she found the door of the house locked and on going to the window to look in, she found a horrible scene. Her grandmother was lying on the floor near the fireplace with her head in a pool of blood, and bending over her was Bryson, holding a dish and striking her lifeless body. No motive was established for the tragedy at the time, as the accused and the victim had been on friendly terms. It was discovered later that the woman had been beaten with a jelly jar, a poker and a hammer by Bryson following a quarrel between them. At his trial, Bryson had entered a special plea of temporary insanity at the time of the murder. A police officer who gave evidence stated that there had been a good deal of blood in the room, splattered four or five feet up the wall. During the course of the trial, Bryson changed his plea to guilty of culpable homicide, which was accepted by the court. He was sentenced to ten years' penal servitude.

15 JULY

1845 The body of a poorly dressed female, thought to be about forty years old, was found in the river, near to Pollockshaws. It was not known how the woman got into the water, or whether she had the intention of killing herself, but she had been observed the previous day in the neighbourhood of the place where her body was found. Her head was found to be severely cut when taken out of the water.

16 JULY

1845   A 'most shameful exhibition' was witnessed at the end of the Glasgow Bridge. During the herring fishing season, the bridge was frequented by the Glasgow fishwives to procure their supplies from the boats. On this particular occasion, several of the women had quarrelled and a battle had ensued with much 'bawling and screaming'. One of the women, having gotten hold of 'a more feeble specimen', beneath her arm, was said to have 'pummelled the unfortunate victim in a most unmerciful manner'. The husband of the weaker woman came forward to help her, only to be attacked by the larger husband of the other woman.

17 JULY

1928   On this date, George Reynolds, sentenced to death at Glasgow High Court the previous month following his conviction for murder, found out that his appeal had failed and the death sentence was to stand. Reynolds had been found guilty of murdering Thomas Lee, a boiler fireman employed at Lang's Bread Co, Wesleyan Street, by striking him with a branding iron. The purpose of the attack seemed to have been robbery, as Reynolds afterwards proceeded to steal the man's scarf, a small sum of money and his overalls. The basis for the appeal had been that the jury were said to have been ill informed that they had the option of delivering a verdict of culpable homicide, if they felt the murder was not premeditated. Additionally, it was reported that the evidence of witnesses had been contradictory. Reynolds' had maintained that he had gone to Lee's work with him in order to assist him in keeping his job, due to him being drunk and unable to perform his duties, during which time Lee had awoken from his drunken sleep, accusing Reynolds of trying to do him out of his job and threatened him with a shovel. Reynolds' account of the matter was doubted by the appeal judges, and despite the culpable homicide question, maintained that he should face the death penalty.

18 JULY

1856   A cabinetmaker named James McCulloch, residing in Stockwell Street, was convicted at the Police Court of having 'committed a wanton and unprovoked assault' on Mrs Buchanan, the wife of a flesher. It appeared that McCulloch, while in a state of intoxication, ejected his wife and stepson in their night dresses, from his house. Mrs Buchanan, observing this, went and asked him for their clothes, at which point he rushed out, knocked her down and kicked her whilst she was on the ground. He was sentenced to sixty days' imprisonment.

Glasgow Bridge, *c.* 1912.

19 JULY

1844   At about four o'clock in the afternoon, while Thomas Frew, a carrier, was receiving some goods, his horse ran off down a narrow street. A woman named Mrs Tannock had just stepped onto the street with a six-month-old child in her arms as the horse was passing. Either by the horse or the cart coming into contact with the child, it was knocked to the ground, dying about an hour afterwards. Mrs Tannock was also crushed, her arm broken and her head seriously injured. It appeared that Frew had requested a young lad of about fourteen years old to take charge of his horse, but he had carelessly gone away.

20 JULY

1895   A double murder, followed by the suicide of the murderer, was reported in the newspapers on this date. On a previous evening in Glasgow, a woman named Milroy, residing in Vernon Street, Maryhill, cut the throats of her two children with a razor and inflicted wounds described as 'instantaneously fatal'. The woman then committed suicide in the same manner using the same weapon, later dying in hospital from her injuries. One child was aged six weeks and the other, sixteen months. It was reported that the woman had suffered from insanity.

21 JULY

1826 An old woman was found by some children, lying dead at the door of a garret room, which she had occupied in the High Street. She had not been seen for some days, and from the state of the decomposition of the body, it was supposed that she had lay dead in front of her dwelling for that period.

22 JULY

1844 A report appeared in the newspapers of a woman and three children, the youngest less that a year old, lying on the pavement in Candleriggs Street in a 'state of great destitution', the woman and one of the children being evidently unwell. The police officer who found them had taken them all to the police office and sent word to the Town's Hospital. Upon enquiry, it was found that the woman and her children had been brought into the city by a Hamilton carrier named Leggate, who had left them there to fend for themselves. Legatte was brought before the magistrate to state where he had brought the woman and her children from. He told the court that he had brought them from a lodging house in Hamilton at the request of Mr Simpson, the manager of the poor for that town, adding that he had done this many times before. It emerged that the woman had been destitute since her husband had died nine months prior to this, and had recently contracted typhus fever. An enquiry was ordered into the proceedings of Mr Simpson.

23 JULY

1852 At the Southern Police Court, a man named Daniel Cameron was charged with a 'disgraceful assault'. Having gone home 'the worse for liquor', he began to quarrell with his wife, who, at the time, had their young child in her arms. In order to get revenge against the mother, he took the infant and hit it several times against the wall, then threw it on the floor. He was sentenced to sixty days in prison.

24 JULY

1826 A rug dealer named Peter Hogg was brought before the court, charged with being drunk and disorderly in his own house in Alston Street. Hogg had assaulted, struck and kicked his wife, to her serious injury 'and the disturbance of the neighbourhood'. From the evidence given, it appeared that his wife, in order to preserve her life, had jumped out of the window. Not content with this, Hogg then proceeded to assault a constable, who had arrived to apprehend him, with a poker. He was fined £2 2s.

25 JULY

1845 As sailor James McFarlane was walking peaceably along at the Flesher's Haugh in the Green with a female, he was brutally attacked by a group of Irish men. After knocking him down, kicking him and hitting him about the head and face, his cries of 'murder' fortunately attracted the attention of some individuals in the neighbourhood. With the assistance of the officer of the Green, they managed to take the assailants into custody, while McFarlane, who had received a severe cut on the head, was semi-conscious for some time. In court, the magistrate described the crime as 'the most wantonly cruel assault that had ever come before the court.' The attackers were all fined two guineas each.

26 JULY

1850 The daughter of a house painter named Edwin, residing in Portugal Street, died under 'very melancholy circumstances'. The girl, who was about eight years old, was playing in the next tenement with her friend, whilst the friend's parents were absent. The girls, in looking in the cupboard, discovered a bottle of whisky, which they began to drink. Edwin's daughter, who had taken more whisky than the other girl, then fell into a drowsy state and remained that way until the adults arrived back later that day. Despite obtaining medical assistance, the poor girl died the following morning.

27 JULY

1821 Samuel Warren, who had recently been convicted of resetting stolen goods, was brought out of jail, escorted by a strong party of the city and police officers, the latter holding drawn cutlasses in their hands. Warren, who was accompanied by the common executioner, was tied to the back of a cart and led through the streets of the city. A large printed label was attached to his back, containing the words 'Convicted of resetting stolen goods from a boy'. A huge crowd turned out to see him pass, among them the boy who had stolen the goods in question, until he was recognised by some of the police.

28 JULY

1865 Dr Edward William Pritchard, the Glasgow poisoner, suffered 'the extreme penalty of the law' for the murder by poison of his wife and mother-in-law. The execution was carried out at the foot of the Saltmarket. Pritchard's poisoning of his wife had been a cruel and painful process lasting a period of three months. Using his medical knowledge of the use and effects of poisons, he administered small doses of tartarised antimony and aconite in his wife's food, in an attempt to make it look like a long and lingering illness from some natural cause.

Suspicions were aroused when Mrs Pritchard, accompanied by her eldest daughter, went to Edinburgh on a visit to her parent's house, spending several days during which her health significantly improved. A couple of months later, Mrs Pritchard's mother came to Glasgow to be with her daughter as she had become very ill again. Being in the way, however, she soon fell victim to the acts of the poisoner. She died suddenly and a post-mortem showed the presence of large amounts of antimony and aconite in her body, which was proved to have been administered by her son-in-law, in a preparation of opium called Battley's solution, which the old lady was in the habit of using. During his trial, Pritchard tried to turn the blame onto a servant named Mary McLeod, but later whilst in prison he admitted his guilt. The excitement in the city on the day of execution was described as 'intense', with print shops swarmed with purchasers of publications of various descriptions featuring songs and portraits of the criminal. A huge crowd attended the execution, with people from far and wide arriving in Glasgow by train for the event.

29 JULY **1853** At around half past eight o'clock in the evening, a woman in the western district of the town sent her thirteen-year-old daughter to the shop of a medical man in Main Street, Anderston, for one halfpenny worth of tincture of rhubarb for her infant child. However, instead of the tincture of rhubarb, the doctor mistakenly handed over laudanum. This drug, on being administered to the infant, caused the child to fall into a deep sleep from which it could not be roused. The child died the following morning.

30 JULY **1855** As a young lad named Patrick Duffy was working close to a revolving shaft in a sugar factory, the shaft caught hold of his apron and whirled him round several times, hitting his face violently against the floor. The machinery was stopped straight away and medical assistance was obtained, but the injuries were so severe that he died half an hour afterwards.

31 JULY **1856** Two little girls, described as 'half-starved' were placed at the Police Court bar, charged with begging. The policeman on the King

A drawing of a
Victorian child begging.

Street beat had found them the previous day, going from door to door begging. The girls told the constable that they were hungry as their parents would not give them any food. Knowing that the parents were perfectly able to provide for their children, the constable summoned them to the police office. They were ordered to bring up their children properly or meet the expense of putting the girls to the Reformatory School.

AUGUST

Glasgow Cathedral.

1 AUGUST

1851 In the Central Police Court, two Irishmen named Donnelly and Mulholland, were charged with having struck a cow feeder named Hamilton on the head with a poker, in Jail Square, causing severe injury. Both men denied the charge, but after the examination of witnesses, the charge was proven against Donnelly. He was sentenced to thirty days in the Bridewell.

2 AUGUST

1852 A woman named Sarah Kelly was charged in the Gorbals Police Court, with assaulting her young daughter Jessie, whilst under the influence of drink. For many years Sarah Kelly had 'led such a dissolute life' that her husband had eventually left her. Her three daughters, it was noted were, despite their circumstances, 'enabled to maintain themselves in a respectable manner' and assist their mother as well as they could. However, as Sarah Kelly's behaviour became unbearable, they had all left the house and taken lodgings for themselves. Since doing so, they had been continually harassed by their mother seeking money. On the day of the assault, she had sent the youngest child, Jessie, to one of the others to ask for money. When the girl returned having been unsuccessful, her mother brutally beat her. Sarah Kelly was sentenced to sixty days in the Bridewell.

3 AUGUST

1850 The report of a 'melancholy railway accident' appeared in the newspapers on this date. In the tunnel between Queen Street station and Cowlairs, a fatal accident occurred. James Boyd, an employee who had charge of the stationary engine at Cowlairs, had been at the Queen Street station just before eight o'clock at night, and was due to take his place in one of the trucks on the train that left on the hour, to go home. However, at eleven o'clock on the same night, he was found on one of the rails with his right leg completely severed from his body and the ground around him completely saturated with blood. It was thought that he must have fallen over on the line. Despite his injuries, he was still alive when found, but died during the course of the night, in the Royal Infirmary.

4 AUGUST

1826 In the Police Court, George Seymour, a journeyman shoemaker, was charged with having 'barbarously thrown his wife out of a window', which was three storeys up, in the Trongate. The woman had been taken to hospital with a fractured spine and severe injuries to other parts of her body. However, after an investigation

A steam train similar to the one which killed James Boyd.

into the case, George Seymour was acquitted after it was ascertained that he had been in bed when his wife had been sleepwalking and had fallen out the window.

5 AUGUST   1850   At about six o'clock in the evening, a man named James Divine lost his life in the High Street by being run over by a loaded cart, whilst he was in a state of intoxication. At the time, David Scott, a carter, was proceeding down the street leading two horses with loaded carts. He was at the head of the first horse, and had a firm hold of the reins of both horses. However, when he was passing the Bell o' the Brae, Divine staggered out of a public house and fell before the wheel of the first cart, which passed over his chest from the lower ribs on his right side, to the left shoulder, killing him instantly.

The Trongate.

6 AUGUST | **1861** At about eight o'clock at night, Robert Pattison, an inspector of the poor, went to the Northern Police Office in an inebriated state. No reason could be ascertained for his arriving there, such was the extent of his drunkenness; however, on spotting Captain Nelson, the superintendent of the northern division, he asked to see him. As Captain Nelson was busy and could not see him until later, he ordered that Pattison be locked up in the meantime for his own protection.

At about midnight, a 'barbarous murder' which had been committed in Caithness Street by a man who had cut his own child's throat, was reported to the police. Mr Nelson, arriving at the scene, found the dead body of the infant lying in a bed in the single room which formed the dwelling house, her throat cut from ear to ear and the head almost severed from the body. On enquiring to who the suspected murderer was, Mr Nelson heard the name 'Pattison' and at once remembered the man in the police office.

Accordingly, Pattison was examined at the police office, and on his shirt, blood marks were found. The murder weapon, which had been found at the house, was a razor which had both sides clotted with blood. It was found partially hidden in the bed, and near it, a bloodstained towel was also found, which seemed to have been used by Pattison to wipe his hands after washing them of the blood. It was reported that Pattison's wife had died three weeks before this terrible event, and since then he had been drinking hard. There were two other children in the house, aged three and ten years old. The youngest was Pattison's child and the other was his step child. Neighbours, who had been helping out, became concerned on the night in question, after finding the ten-year-old sitting on the stairs outside, and entered the house. The shocking sight of the dead infant, called Magdeline, was then discovered, and in the corner of the room, the three-year-old was sitting, crying. When asked what had happened, the child told the police that she had seen her father cutting Magdeline in the bed.

7 AUGUST

1846   Early in the morning, a man who had spent the previous night in a respectable tavern in Broomielaw Street, was found dead in his bed. A small bottle was found in his possession, marked 'Laudanum – Poison', and it was ascertained that he had purchased the poison from a shop in Jamaica Street the day before.

8 AUGUST

1851   At the Central Police Court, James Fitzpatrick was charged with 'a very aggravated' assault on his wife, in their house in Bridgegate. In addition to the marks of violence on her body, it had been found that she had been severely burned on the back. Mrs Fitzpatrick, however, denied in court that the burning was caused by her husband, stating that she had fallen on the fireplace. A neighbour, Mrs Campbell, who lived in the same tenement, gave evidence that she had been repeatedly disturbed during the night by noises coming from their house and hearing cries of 'murder'. When Mrs Campbell went to the house, she found Mrs Fitzpatrick lying in the middle of the floor with James Fitzpatrick standing over her with his knee on her chest. He had hold of her by the hair and was knocking her head repeatedly on the floor. Mrs Campbell also told the court that Mrs Fitzpatrick had stated at the time that she had been dragged across the fire. James Fitzpatrick was sentenced to sixty days' imprisonment.

9 AUGUST

1850   As the Milngavie coach was passing one of the city omnibuses during the morning near City Road, a passenger named Alexander Duncan, who was 'a little the worse of liquor', suddenly leaped off and fell back on the street, when the wheels of the omnibus came into contact with, and went right over his body. He was taken to the Royal Infirmary with injuries so severe that he later died.

10 AUGUST

1846   A young man named Archibald Robertson, whilst walking along the street, observed a man who was being taken to the Royal Infirmary with wounds that could be seen flowing with blood. Unfortunately, Robertson had been prone to fainting at the sight of blood and on seeing this injured man, started to feel light-headed. Robertson at once proceeded towards his own house which was nearby, but on ascending the stairs he fell backwards and landed at the very bottom. Robertson sustained a clot in the brain, which he died from a few days later.

11 AUGUST

1851   Jean Muir was charged at the Central Police Court with 'creating a prodigious sensation in Frederick Lane, while under the influence of liquor'. It appeared that Jean had stationed herself at a window of one of the houses in the lane, from which she hurled a great variety of articles, including bottles, plates and other dangerous objects at passers by. Police finally managed to enter the house and put a stop to the odd behaviour, after a shower of boiling water was poured out of the window on the people below. She was sentenced to sixty days' imprisonment.

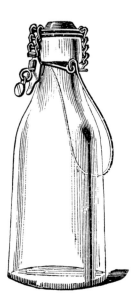

12 AUGUST

1891   In Gairbraid Street in Maryhill, a 'shocking tragedy' occurred. Shortly after two o'clock, when the street was very busy with people, a man named David Gray shot a woman named Nellie Gabriel, the wife of a showman in the city. Gray and Mrs Gabriel had known each other for some time, and had met the previous day and called at a farm in the neighbourhood where Mrs Gabriel's sister resided. Afterwards, they asked if they could spend the night at the farm, but this was refused, so the couple spent the night in a shed. The next day, as they were crossing Gairbraid Street, Mrs Gabriel had stooped down to save her dress from the mud, and at that moment Gray took the revolver from his pocket and without a word of warning, shot her. Before the passers-by could recover from the shock of what had happened, Gray placed the revolver behind his right ear and blew out his own brains. A letter was found in Gray's pocket, addressed to his son, stating that he would never see him again and telling him, 'Nellie goes out of this life with me. I have a revolver loaded.'

13 AUGUST **1925** In a tenement building in Marquis Street, in the East End of Glasgow, a 'distressing tragedy' was reported, in which a two-year-old girl and a four-year-old boy were murdered. An iron turner who had went there to visit his sister, Louisa Lawson, a twenty-four-year-old widow, made the shocking discovery. When his sister let him in, the man found the youngest child, Elizabeth Lawson, on the bed with her throat cut and Joseph Lawson, bleeding profusely from a severe wound on his throat. The boy was taken to the Royal Infirmary, but died within two hours of admission. Louisa Lawson was apprehended for murder. It was reported that she had been receiving an allowance from the Parish Council since the death of her husband, but had supplemented this income by knitting jumpers for her friends. Shortly before the incident, Mrs Lawson had been quarrelling with a neighbour who had been slow in making payments for a jumper that she had knitted for her. The neighbour in response, had threatened to tell the Parish Council that Mrs Lawson was earning money from knitting, so that her allowance would be stopped. Mrs Lawson, who had already been in low spirits since the death of her mother earlier in the year, had been upset by the neighbours' actions and was worried about the loss of her income.

At the trial, Mrs Lawson's brother, Julius Luth, told the court that when he went to the house on the day of the incident, she had pointed to the children on the bed and exclaimed, 'Look what I have

Newspaper headline around the time of the shooting of Nellie Gabriel.

DREADFUL TRAGEDY IN GLASGOW.

done.' He had noticed a strong smell of gas at the time and it was supposed that Mrs Lawson had intended to take her own life after killing the children. This was supported by the evidence of Mr Luth's wife who told the court she had been given a letter by Mrs Lawson which read, 'Maggie, please see to everything for me. I am taking this way out of my trouble ... Do not let them say I am insane; I'm not. I've nobody; I'm better away with my children'. The medical evidence presented to the trial pointed to Mrs Lawson being insane at the time of the crime, with Professor Glaiser of Glasgow University telling the court that 'he had no doubt that the woman's mind was entirely upset'. The jury returned a verdict that the accused had committed the crime, but was insane at the time of the act. Louisa Lawson was sentenced to be detained indefinitely at Her Majesty's pleasure.

14 AUGUST   1805   Four-year-old Alexander Thomson, whilst in Trongate Street, was severely bitten on the face by a dog. The dog was not thought to have been carrying any disease and Alexander's wounds eventually healed. However, after a few months, he began to complain of headaches, sickness and loss of appetite, with signs of 'hyrophobia', otherwise known as rabies, starting to show. The young boy was treated with 'repeated effusions of salt and water'; however, the disease spread rapidly and he died a few days after the initial symptoms showed. Around this time, there had been three other cases of rabies in the same neighbourhood.

A Victorian cartoon on the subject of rabies.

15 AUGUST

1853 Hans MacFarlane and Helen Blackwood, convicted of the murder of ships carpenter Alexander Boyd in the New Vennel, 'suffered the last sentence of the law' on this date. The place of execution had been in front of the South Prison at Jail Square. It was reported that during the course of the morning, the arrival of spectators was continuous right up until the time of the execution, with it estimated that 23,000 people had been in attendance, the majority of which were said to 'belong to the sphere of life in which the criminals had moved'. Police stood all around the sides of the scaffold, but had difficulty in keeping the strong crowd of spectators within the prescribed boundaries. It was reported that the night before the execution MacFarlane had only slept for a very short time, getting up at three o'clock in the morning, whilst Blackwood had slept all night, only getting out of her bed at seven o'clock.

In the morning, both prisoners met for the first time since their conviction and partook of a cup of tea and a glass of wine each, before being taken into the Court Hall. MacFarlane was said to have 'walked firmly into the Hall, whereas Blackwood, 'looking weak and emaciated' had to be assisted. The execution itself was conducted very quickly, with the bodies only struggling a few minutes. MacFarlane and Blackwood, who were in a relationship, had 'rented and occupied a wretched hovel' in the same tenement in which they committed the murder. In this 'hovel', which was basically one room, three men, three women and two children lived, a circumstance which was not uncommon during this time. A few months prior to Alexander Boyd's murder, another man had been lured to this hovel and robbed of his belongings. The culprits were not brought to justice for this, although it was suspected that MacFarlane and Blackwood had also been responsible for this crime.

16 AUGUST

1850 In the village of Govan, a serious accident occurred at the dye works, by which a young woman named Marion Stewart, lost both her feet above the ankles. Marion, who was a servant employed by a spirit dealer, had crossed over the Clyde to fetch some hot water from the dye house, when she went too near the machinery. Her clothes becoming entangled, she was dragged into the wheels, where her feet were both cut off and her legs mangled.

17 AUGUST

1820 Early in the morning, whilst a workman and his wife were in their garden, a neighbour had gone into their house to get some kindling for her fire. As it was difficult to get the light inflamed, another neighbour came in to help. As the owner of the house had previously been employed in blasting rocks, a canister containing two pounds of blasting powder was present in the room. Taking this canister, the neighbour managed to get a light, but unfortunately a spark fell into the container, which he had placed between his knees. As the explosion took place, the woman of the house had been making her way indoors, with her husband behind her. She was thrown back with the force of the blast and knocked over her husband. The doors of the house were forced from their hinges and shattered to pieces, the windows blown out and the house was unroofed in two places. All parties present were burned to some degree and bruised, but all survived. However, it was also discovered that during all the confusion of the blast, a watch and several other articles had been stolen from the house by some opportunistic persons.

18 AUGUST

1826 About eight o'clock at night, a 'novel method of robbing' occurred in the east of the city. While a young man was on his way home, he was accosted by three men near the Gallowgate Toll, who asked him how far he had to go. On telling them he was going to Langloan, the men said they were going his way too and appearing friendly, offered him a drink out of a bottle they had in their possession. After taking a drink, he soon started to feel strange, but took up an offer of the three men to go into a public house to have some whisky, into which they poured a portion of the liquid in the bottle. The young man gradually grew more weak and drowsy and was assisted to a haystack on the roadside. Once there, the men stripped him of all his clothes and robbed him of his watch and some silver. The owner of the haystack discovered him in the morning in a state of nudity, shivering with cold.

19 AUGUST

1853 A young man was brought before the Central Police Court on the charge of 'drunkenness'. A compositor by trade, the young man was respectably connected and had 'a genteel appearance and manners'. However, he had become 'addicted to drinking' and had regularly been brought to the police office in a state of intoxication. On one occasion his drunkenness had led to him cutting his own throat when he was refused admission to a brothel.

20 AUGUST

Areas of Glasgow - The Gorbals

This area, on the south bank of the River Clyde, was by the end of the nineteenth century, suffering from the same population increases as other Glasgow areas, due to the industrialisation that had occurred throughout the city. The area had become known as a dangerous place and many people living there experienced slum conditions, The City Improvement Trust attempted to help this situation by clearing some of the slum tenements in 1866, which included the demolition of Main Street. Jewish, Irish and Italian immigrants made the Gorbals their home during the nineteenth century and early twentieth century, attracted to the area by the wave of new industrial jobs. The Gorbals railway station opened in 1877; however, it closed to passengers in 1928 due to a lack of business following changes in the area.

21 AUGUST

1852   At the Central Police Court, a man named Young appeared on a charge of assaulting his wife. It appeared from the evidence that for some time past, Young had been 'leading a dissolute life' and whenever drunk, would go home and carry away clothes and furniture in order to pawn them. On the day of the assault, he had been about to do the same when an argument ensued with his wife, whom he struck violently on the head. In court, the woman had appeared pale and emaciated, stating that the only money coming into their household was her small earnings from needlework. Young was sentenced to thirty days in the Bridewell.

22 AUGUST

1844   An old man named Malcolm appeared at the Gorbals Police Court on a charge of 'reckless conduct'. Malcolm, who owned a property in Clyde Terrace and a small green in front of it, near to the river side, was tried and convicted of using a horsewhip towards a child, in such a manner that the little boy, who had been playing near the edge of the river, was so frightened that he tumbled over the wall into the bed of the river, almost drowning. Malcolm, who had previously been convicted of other assaults on children, was fined £1.

23 AUGUST

1844   Whilst the Great Cattle Show was taking place, a number of people climbed up on a wall which separated the Green from a private property on the north side, in order to have a better view of the cattle. Suddenly and without warning, a pistol, which appeared to have been loaded with slag, was discharged from within the garden of the property, immediately after which someone was seen to hastily enter the house. However, the description of the perpetrator had been inconclusive, as some witnesses spoke of seeing a lady and others said it was a man wearing what looked like a turban. The police, who came immediately on hearing the shot, entered the premises and found an elderly lady there, standing at a mirror, and fitting a bonnet upon her head. She, however, denied all knowledge of the incident, and a search of the property failed to turn up the pistol. An elderly male servant of the house was also questioned, who also denied all knowledge of the matter. Five or six people were wounded by the shot, two of them boys, one no more than six or seven years old. The older boy, about ten years old, was taken to the police office, where several slugs were extracted from his arm by the surgeon. Having failed to find the culprit, it was thought the act could not be the work of 'any one but a lunatic'.

24 AUGUST

1821 Mary Campbell, who had been under the sentence of 'banishment' from the city, turned up in the Trongate and managed to lure a four-year-old girl into a close. There, Campbell 'stripped her to the skin' and left her. She was apprehended the next morning and identified by the child.

25 AUGUST

Areas of Glasgow - High Street

Originally the main street of the city, High Street connected the north and south banks of the River Clyde. Until 1870, the original buildings of Glasgow University were located at the junction of this street and Duke Street, prior to their relocation to the west end of the city. However, the nineteenth-century Industrial Revolution, which caused considerable growth in the size of the city, led to High Street losing some of its previous importance, as the City Chambers, among other important buildings moved elsewhere. The wynds and closes around the High Street became synonymous with overcrowding and unsanitary conditions during the nineteenth century, although efforts were being made to try and alleviate some of these problems, with the report of the Sanitary Inspector in 1897 noting that the area, 'through the radical rooting out of unsanitary blocks of dwellings and the introduction of sanitary improvements in those which remain, is taking a higher position both with respect to death rate from all causes and from infectious diseases'. Prior to this an article in the *Glasgow Herald* on 'The condition of Glasgow – the wynds and closes' described the conditions in the area following an inspection:

> Situated on both sides of the High Street, these closes may well represent the minute ramifications of vitiated arterial blood... The features were; old, crazy, dilapidated, and sometimes ruinous tenements, teeming with inhabitants of every age and of both sexes. The Pipehouse Close leading off the High Street, was the first examined. The 'lands' here are usually five or six storeys in height.
>
> Most of the apartments, as far as we could guess, were not above nine or ten feet square, and seven or eight feet in height. In such an apartment, sometimes two families ate their meals and slept together. There was not the slightest provision for ventilation; and in some cases there was no provision for light. Of course there was no drainage; and we will not pretend to describe the effect of this in producing surface filth. In one cellar, without a window, we found an old apple woman living. She was nearly eighty years of age. She said in reply to our inquiry, that the place 'was not what she would like', but she added, with a tone of resignation, that she had not very long to live, and that it would last her day. One close is walled in and built over the surrounding and superincumbent buildings; yet the hovels in the close were all crowded with population, chiefly women and children.

26 AUGUST   **1858** At the Central Police Court, a woman named Martha Broadley, the wife of a labourer, was accused of assaulting her eight-year-old daughter. From the evidence of the surgeon, it appeared that the poor little girl had been thrashed with a strap or rope 'until her whole body was covered with black and blue bruises'. From the evidence of other witnesses, it was ascertained that Martha Broadley and her husband had been in the habit of

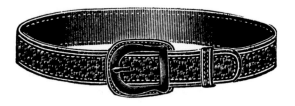

treating their unfortunate children in a similarly brutal manner. She was sentenced to sixty days' imprisonment with hard labour, while a search was made for her husband who had managed to avoid being apprehended.

27 AUGUST

1852   Early in the morning, the wife of a ship watchman, John Hunter, was discovered dead in her bed within their house. Both husband and wife were described as being 'much addicted to intemperance', and they had been seen in a drunken state the previous day, when Hunter had been demanding money from his wife. Later on that night, friends of his who had helped him home after he had consumed even more drink, found the body of Mrs Hunter. It appeared she had died from a wound on the side of her head. John Hunter was taken into custody.

28 AUGUST

1891   Mary Ann Anderson appeared at the Central Police Court on this date, charged with child murder. Her apprehension was the result of a long investigation after a box, which had been lying in the outward cloak room at Queen Street Station and emitting an offensive smell, was finally opened and the body of a female child was found inside. The child's body had been wrapped in a newspaper, then a towel, then a piece of blanket. A post-mortem showed that the baby had been born alive, and that death had been caused by a violent pressure on the infant's chest. Having no information as to the depositor of the box, news about the finding was circulated to the public to try and find the person responsible. As a result, information was given that a woman, who had occupied a single apartment in a house in Crown Street, had left suddenly about the time the box was deposited at the station, having recently given birth to a female child. It was ascertained that the baby had been born four days before the body was left at the station, and the mother had told the midwife that the child's aunt had telegraphed for the infant. The midwife, having given a flannel to keep the baby warm on the journey, identified this flannel as the one the dead child had been wrapped in. After the birth, the mother sold the furniture of her house to a broker and then left the area. On her arrest, she said to the officers, 'I expected it; no one should do evil that good may come out of it.' The thirty-two-year-old Mary Anderson, was a widow, her husband having died four years previously, leaving her with two girls, aged four and seven at the time of the murder. Having placed the girls in a home, she had become pregnant after being involved with a man, and facing the prospect of bringing up an illegitimate child, she gave the reason for the murder as an attempt to prevent reproach falling on her husband's daughters.

29 AUGUST   **1848** Late in the evening, an assault was committed by a man named Miller upon his wife at their home in Piccadilly Street. Whilst Miller was asleep, his wife had taken a small sum of money from his pocket, and when he awoke and found the money missing, he lifted a poker and struck her on the head. Mrs Miller fell to the floor, bleeding profusely, her scalp 'having been laid open'. In court, Mrs Miller spoke up for her husband, stating that he was very kind to her when sober. As a result, he was fined 10s.

30 AUGUST   **1852** Whilst two boys were amusing themselves by searching through a cellar in Smith's Court, Candleriggs Street, they discovered the body of a male child wrapped in a piece of blue flannel. On examination, the child appeared to have been born alive, but the body was very much decomposed. The circumstances surrounding the how the body came to be there, or how long it had been there, could not be established.

31 AUGUST   **1852** Hugh McIlvainey, described as 'a rascal', was sentenced to thirty days' imprisonment at the Central Police Court for robbing a child in Gallowgate Street. McIlvaney had stolen the sum of 2½d from the child, who was four years old.

SEPTEMBER

Charing Cross, Glasgow.

1 SEPTEMBER   **1853** A thirty-year-old married woman, whose husband had deserted her and went to America, committed suicide in her father's house where she had been residing. It was reported that for some time she had been 'addicted to drink to an extent that occasionally affected her mind'. At four o'clock in the afternoon, she had remained in the house alone, while her relations went out, and when they returned around eight o'clock in the evening, she was found lying on a bed on the floor with her throat cut 'nearly from ear to ear' and a razor lying beside her.

2 SEPTEMBER   **Glasgow Institutions – The Town Hospital and the City Poorhouse:**
A system of poor relief was established in Glasgow and other cities in the nineteenth century, which in Glasgow, had originally made use of the Town Hospital to accommodate the 'deserving and infirm poor' of the city. Places were limited, however, and in 1815, measures were taken to clamp down on able-bodied beggars and paupers from outside of the city being given relief. By 1843, the hospital buildings had become inadequate for their purposes and the old Royal Lunatic Asylum buildings in Parliamentary Road were utilised instead as a poorhouse. Glasgow, with its rapidly expanding population, had a large number of 'paupers' at this time, living in the slum areas and low lodging houses. Parochial Boards, who assessed the applications for relief, used strict criteria in determining whether an application should be approved. An illness or disability which prevented a person from obtaining work and supporting themselves would normally be the main reason for approving relief, and a medical examination would be carried out on the applicant. In the event of relief being granted, the committee would then decide whether the person was eligible to receive 'outdoor relief', in other words living in their homes but receiving financial support, or whether they should be admitted to the poorhouse.

The poorhouse was always seen as a last resort by people, as these institutions tended to be harsh, unwelcoming places where only the truly destitute would want to seek refuge. Hospital buildings were often used for this purpose, due to the simplicity of being able to transfer ill people in the poorhouse to the wards should they need treatment, which they often did due to poverty and disease going hand in hand. This treatment was not automatically given to those receiving outdoor relief however. Due to issues of cost, the standard of medical care and treatment in the poorhouses was not particularly high. In fact, the City poorhouse only began using antiseptic many years after it had been used routinely in the Royal Infirmary. Surgery was regularly carried out on the overcrowded wards up until the end of the nineteenth century, in view of other patients. Overcrowding was a big issue and there were reports of hospital inmates having to share beds and poorhouse inmates being accommodated on the wards, even though they were not ill. In 1898, however, following a merger with the Barony parishes, the city facility was closed down and the poor were sent to Barnhill Poorhouse. The hospital wards were also separated from the facility when Poor Law hospitals began to be built in 1902.

3 SEPTEMBER   **1847**   At the Gorbals Police Court, two women and two men were tried before the magistrate for 'a dangerous and reckless assault with a bottle and their fists on the person of a poor dumb man' in Rutherglen Loan. As a result of the attack, the man had been severely cut and injured. After hearing witnesses, the charge was found to be proved and the women were fined 10s each, whilst the men were fined one guinea each.

4 SEPTEMBER   **1846**   At the chemical works of C.M. Payne, one of the workmen was removing a boiling liquid from a large open boiler, when he accidentally lost his footing and fell in. He scrambled out before assistance arrived, but from the severe scalding he received, he died the following day in the Infirmary.

5 SEPTEMBER   **1858**   A report in the *Glasgow Herald* featured the case of Ann Rownie, who had been 'engaged in some domestic pursuit' and sustained a very severe burn from the shoulder to the wrist of her right arm, caused by the sleeve of her dress catching fire. Her arm being described as being 'literally roasted', she was admitted to the Infirmary, when on the tenth day of her stay, the symptoms of lockjaw became apparent. After thirty-six hours of agony, the forty-two-year-old woman died.

6 SEPTEMBER   **1890**   At the High Court of Justiciary held in Glasgow, Thomas Gribbin was charged with having stabbed and murdered Michael Kane in a house in Saltmarket. Having pleaded not guilty, the case went to trial. Gribbin, who had been a lodger in Kane's house, had a quarrel about money which was supposedly owed in rent.

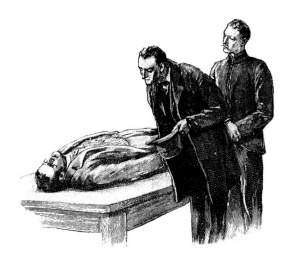

A newspaper clipping detailing events of Michael Kane's murder.

MURDER TRIAL AT GLASGOW.
SENTENCE OF DEATH.

Kane got into bed, but the quarrel between the two men, both under the influence of alcohol, continued. Gribbin had been seen by Mrs Kane, leaning over her husband in the bed, then walking away and sitting by the fireside. Immediately going over to her husband, she found that he had been killed. A knife was later found beneath the pillow. The post-mortem showed that an incised wound an inch in length on the right side of the chest had been the cause of death. The jury, after retiring for fifteen minutes, returned with a unanimous verdict of guilty. Gribbin, who showed no emotion at the verdict, was sentenced to be executed within the walls of Glasgow Prison on the 24 September.

7 SEPTEMBER Glasgow Institutions – Barnhill Poorhouse

The poorhouse was officially opened in the 1850s, and was known in the mid-to-late nineteenth century for its harsh regime and bad conditions. Inmates would be fed, washed and their belongings de-loused on arrival, then if they were able bodied, they would be expected to carry out rigorous physical work, such as making up bundles of firewood and breaking stones, for which they were not paid. It was reported at the time that the standard of food served to inmates was of a very poor quality, with inmates who did not carry out the required amount of work for the day being placed on a diet of bread and water and placed in solitary confinement. Any disorderly conduct also resulted in a restriction of food. Following the merger in 1898 with the Glasgow City Porhouse, Barnhill became the largest poorhouse in Scotland. There were some who campaigned to improve conditions, however, with some success. A report on Barnhill Poorhouse in 1876 reflected on the previous conditions experienced there and the attitude of the poorhouse management:

> We have a lively remembrance of what took place some eleven years ago, when the exposures were made of overcrowding, pauper nursing, ill treatment and general sanitary deficiencies, that prevailed in our workhouse hospital, and how virulently the several Boards of Guardians implicated in the wrong-doing attacked those who had been instrumental in bringing the subject before the public, and how recklessly and audaciously they denied the truth of the allegations which were brought against their management.

8 SEPTEMBER   **1848**   At the Southern District Police Court, Owen Banachan and Mary Wood were charged with assaulting a married woman named Mary Eichan. It appeared that Banachan's wife had quarrelled with Eichan in Rutherglen Loan and the argument had escalated to blows being exchanged. Banachan interfered and, assisted by his stepdaughter Mary Wood, seized hold of Eichan and held her down on the street while his wife struck her several times on the head with a hatchet. The incident created quite a commotion in the street, but before the police could arrive, the main assailant had left the scene. Banachan and his stepdaughter were lodged in the Gorbals Police Office until their court appearance, when they were convicted and sentenced to sixty days' imprisonment and thirty days' imprisonment respectively.

9 SEPTEMBER   **1848**   A young girl, residing in Clyde Terrace, attempted to commit suicide by swallowing a small quantity of arsenic. Having purchased the poison from a druggist under the pretence that she wanted to kill rats, she returned home and immediately swallowed the dose, then on leaving the house, she went and lay down in Carlton Green. Although she was found and taken to receive medical assistance, she later died from the effects of the poison.

10 SEPTEMBER 1852   A seaman named McFarlane was placed at the bar of the Central Police Court, charged with 'riotous and disorderly conduct' as well as assault. Described as 'an idle fellow', McFarlane had been out of employment for nine months and was dependant on his two sisters and his widowed mother. Having come home one evening and demanded 2s from one of his sisters, who refused to give up such a large proportion of her hard-earned money, he attacked her. His mother then intervened, but was pushed to the ground and also assaulted. The charge was found to be proved and McFarlane was sentenced to sixty days' imprisonment.

11 SEPTEMBER 1855   A middle-aged man named William Martin, an iron dresser from Cowcaddens Street, was charged with having assaulted his mother and brother whilst 'in a state of intoxication'. During the incident he had also pursued, and threatened to stab, his sister Helen. Martin was ordered to pay a fine of three guineas, which he did not have, therefore he was sent to prison for sixty days.

12 SEPTEMBER 1845   During an argument between Belinda Boyce and Letitia McCann, a serious injury was received by McCann in her house in Dale Street, Bridgeton. Boyce, filled with rage, picked up a bowl containing scalding porridge and threw it in the face of McCann. The bowl broke over her face and she was severely wounded by the hot porridge. Boyce pleaded guilty, but stated that she had carried out the act 'under circumstances of great provocation', and was sentenced to one month's imprisonment.

13 SEPTEMBER 1835   On this date, George Campbell appeared in court charged with murdering Mary Watters in her own house in Deacon's Close, by knocking her to the ground, kicking her and leaping heavily on her body. Mary Armstrong, who lived in Mrs Watters' house, told the court that George Campbell cohabited with Mrs Watters' daughter, and was 'occasionally addicted to drink' and when intoxicated 'he was of a violent temper', and in the habit of striking Mrs Watters and her daughter. On the day in question, Mrs Watters and Campbell

had fallen out in the street and Campbell returned home before her, swearing vengeance against her and stating her would 'take her life' when she came in. After hearing all the evidence, the jury retired for twenty minutes, unanimously finding Campbell guilty. Lord Meadowbank, assuming the black cap, sentenced him to death, at which point Campbell broke into a string of insults and swearing. His Lordship proceeding, said, 'You, wretched being that you are, may think that you may brave it out, but I solemnly warn you that you are standing on the threshold of your fate.' Campbell, who was sentenced to be hanged by the common executioner on the 29 September, was removed from the court amidst the disgust of the spectators.

14 SEPTEMBER 1849 At about two o'clock in the morning, a spirit dealer from Rutherglen Loan, was brought to the Gorbals Police Office charged with assault. The spirit dealer had shut up his premises for the night at the usual hour, after which he was frequently disturbed by people knocking at his door for admission. It seemed that one of these people had knocked again and again at the door of the publican, who having had enough of this annoyance, lifted a sword and stuck the man, nearly severing one of his arms from his body.

15 SEPTEMBER 1854 Whilst the police were taking a man named David Williams into custody for disorderly conduct, he seized hold of a lamp post and 'clung to it with all his might'. The police were attempting to unfasten his arms from the lamp post when he suddenly took a large knife from his pocket and struck out indiscriminately, stabbing a fourteen-year-old boy named George McCann, who happened to be passing by.

16 SEPTEMBER 1850 While a number of boys were playing near the pond at Graham Square Mills, they saw, on the surface of

A Victorian street lamp.

the water, the body of an infant. When the news reached people in the neighbourhood, the body was taken out and found to be that of a male child, which appeared to have been in the water for some time. As heavy metal weights had been attached to both legs of the child for the purpose of sinking the infant, the remains would probably have continued undiscovered if a recent drought hadn't dried up the water to such a degree.

17 SEPTEMBER 1852 During the afternoon, 'whilst under the influence of liquor', an old man named Mathieson was proceeding along the Gallowgate. Stumbling on the kerb of the pavement, Mathieson ended up falling against an asphalt boiler, into which his arm was thrust, becoming encrusted with the boiling contents.

18 SEPTEMBER 1854 At Thomas Kyle and Sons, Cowcaddens Street, an accident involving a 'terrible mutilation' occurred. Christina Colquhoun, twenty-three years old, entered into an area at the back of the works amongst the machinery in order to sweep up, when her clothes got entangled in the machinery whilst it was in motion. Seeing Christina being dragged into the machinery, the engineer rushed over and tried to get her out, at the same time calling to those inside to stop the engine. However, by the time the engine could be stopped, both her legs had been torn off above the knees and one of her arms had been wrenched from her body. Still alive, she was taken to the Infirmary. It would appear that Christina had no need to even be in that area cleaning.

19 SEPTEMBER 1852 A man and a woman were both charged at the Central Police Court with having kept lodging houses 'for the accommodation of mendicants and labourers', without obtaining the required licences. In the house occupied by the man, in a single apartment eight feet square, eight persons were found lying together. They consisted of young and old people, male and female, and they lay there without any covering to keep them warm. In the house occupied by the female, in two small apartments, eighteen persons were found in a similar way. Both parties were fined.

20 SEPTEMBER 1842 Sawyer, John McCrae and his servant were charged with the 'cruel and barbarous treatment' of McCrae's wife, who was 'a person of weak of unsound mind'. The circumstances were that having

fitted a press measuring three feet six inches in length, two feet and a half in breadth and two feet six inches in height, McCrae, assisted by his servant, had kept his wife in there night and day, with the door fixed with a hook and eye. The press contained no bed or covers, and instead was littered with straw on the floor. It was detailed that Mrs McCrae had been kept in a state of nakedness and in a filthy and squalid condition, by which she 'became reduced to a state of idiocy' and lost the power of her limbs. Both accused pleaded not guilty. McCrae's defence was that he was often away from home and had trusted his servant to take proper care of his wife, but the jury, without leaving the box, found him guilty. He was sentenced to one year in prison, whilst the servant was allowed to go free.

21 SEPTEMBER 1808 Fourteen-year-old John Wilson found himself accused of murder after a quarrel with another boy. Wilson, who during the course of the argument, picked up a brick bat and threw it at the other boy, causing his death, stated, 'I did not intend it.' The jury found him guilty of the lesser charge of culpable homicide, and recommended leniency. Wilson was sentenced to one month in Glasgow Jail.

22 SEPTEMBER 1808 James Waddel, accused of assaulting James McClayman, a labourer, by striking him on the left arm with an axe, pleaded not guilty to the charge and the case went to trial. The crime was alleged to have taken place in Waddel's house, and McClayman had been severely cut, losing a lot of blood, which nearly ended in the loss of his life. The jury found the assault proven, but their opinion was that there was no proof Waddel had acted with premeditated malice, therefore leniency was recommended. Waddel was sentenced to two months in the Tolbooth of Glasgow initially, then to be held there afterwards until he paid a fine of £200.

23 SEPTEMBER 1848 Margaret Park was placed at the bar of the Police Court, charged with having 'feloniously stolen a little child named Mary Morrison' and also of having, within her own house in Bell Street, Calton, 'feloniously stripped the clothes off the child' to send them to pawnbrokers in the city. Mrs Morrison, the child's mother, told the court that her daughter had gone out in the afternoon and had not returned. As news of the disappearance spread throughout the neighbourhood, the child's father and another man received information that led them to Margaret Park's house, where they

found the child, stripped of her clothes. After evidence from other witnesses, the jury found Park guilty of both charges and was sentenced to fourteen years' transportation.

24 SEPTEMBER **1823** Mary Horn found herself in court on this date, charged with having assaulted and attempted to murder Janet McLaren, a young deaf and dumb woman, in a house in the High Street. The assault had involved Horn inflicting severe blows on the young woman with a hammer, as a result of which, Janet McLaren died. A witness saw Horn on the day of the incident, threaten Janet, stating 'she would do for her for looking in at her door', after which she was reported to have struck the woman on the head, then lifted a hammer from the fireside and struck her on the head and shoulders. Neighbours intervened and Horn was pulled away from Janet McLaren, who was then taken to the Infirmary, later dying from her injuries. The jury found Mary Horn guilty of the assault, but not of the intent to murder.

25 SEPTEMBER **1925** In Duke Street Prison, John Keen was executed for the murder of 'an Indian pedlar' named Noorh Mohammed. It was reported in the *Scotsman* newspaper that 'a remarkable feature of the proceedings was the attendance at the scaffold of a lady, who was one of the two junior magistrates'. Keen's crime had been to go, along with a number of other men, to a dwelling house in Water Street, and subject the occupants, a number of Indian pedlars 'to considerable violence'. The occupants of the house had been hit with crockery, pieces of wood and other items which the men had thrown. Keen, however, was the person identified by witnesses as being the one who stabbed Noorh Mohammed with a dagger. Half an hour before the

exection, a crowd began to gather in Cathedral Square, outside the northern wall of Duke Street Prison. It was reported that by eight o'clock, 2,000 were present. As the practice of hoisting the black flag after an execution had been abandoned, the crowd eventually began to disperse, assuming that after a suitable period had passed, that the execution had been carried out.

26 SEPTEMBER 1833   A miner and two weavers, who were accused of rape on a woman named Mrs Tennent, were 'outlawed' for not appearing in court. The Lord Justice Clerk said that the individuals outlawed were 'charged with one of the most aggravated cases of rape that had ever come under his observation' and that he hoped the authorities would do everything in their power 'to bring the delinquents to justice'. The term 'outlawry' referred to the formal procedure of declaring someone an outlaw. In other words, putting the person beyond the protection of the law, which meant that they had no legal right to protection from mob justice. It was also a crime for anyone to give such a person shelter. By not appearing in court to answer the accusations, the accused person was guilty of contempt of court, which was a capital crime, therefore even if the person was innocent of the original crime, they were still guilty of evading justice and so would still face a punishment.

27 SEPTEMBER 1822   Edward Hand, who had previously been convicted at the Circuit Court in Glasgow of an assault 'aggravated with the intention of committing a rape upon the body of a young girl', was publicly whipped through the streets of the city, as per the terms of his sentence. He had been brought out of the prison under a strong guard of cavalry, and at the jail he had received twenty lashes, followed by a further twenty at the foot of Stockwell Street, again at the foot of Glassford Street and finally at the Cross, making eighty lashes in total. His back was described as 'much lacerated from the flagellation'. Edward Hand afterwards faced the second part of his sentence, which was transportation for life. Hand had been a married man and his defence at the trial had been that he had embarked upon an 'affair' with the girl and that she had been a willing participant. However, due to her young age of twelve years old, the court had not been sympathetic to his reasoning. Lord Meadowbank on sentencing Hand had sternly told him that if the girl had been any younger, he would have been facing the scaffold for his crime.

28 SEPTEMBER   1858   Helen McAra and Jessie Henderson, two thirteen-year-old girls, were brought up before the sheriff on a charge of malicious mischief or wilful fire raising. Both girls tearfully admitted their guilt. They had both been inmates of the House of Refuge in Parliamentary Road, where they had been sent for committing theft. However, taking a dislike of their new home, they decided to set fire to the premises, hoping to make their escape whilst the gate was opened for the fire engines. In the early hours of the morning, on the date in question, they set fire to their beds and bedding, causing panic amongst the other girls. The two accused were sentenced to thirty days' imprisonment, to be followed by five years back in the House of Refuge.

29 SEPTEMBER   1848   At the new railway station in the Gorbals, Myles Nisbet, a ganger, was present for the opening of the line, for which two cannons had been obtained for the purpose of firing a salute as the train making the directors' trial trip started. As the company were assembling for the trip, Nisbet, along with a number of other workmen was firing off some blank charges as a test. While preparing to fire off one of the guns, Nisbet had put his arms round it in an attempt to raise it, when the gun went off. Being right in front of the gun at the time, Nisbet's right leg and arm were blown off and his body was shattered to pieces.

30 SEPTEMBER   1853   Another 'hotbed of disease' in the form of an overcrowded lodging house, was brought to the attention of the Bailies at the Central Police Court. The 'house' in this instance was a basement flat consisting of two apartments containing nine beds, nine men, ten women and eight children. The lodging house keeper, James Kelly, was fined half a guinea.

OCTOBER

Looking east from Argyle Street.

1 OCTOBER   **1852**   In the Cowcaddens district, two men named Sweeney, a father and son, had gone to the police office to settle their differences after having quarrelled in their lodgings. With this quarrel settled they went on their way. However, young Sweeney found that on returning home, he was denied admission by his landlord. Sweeney persisted, and the landord, a man named Gougain, became irritated with Sweeney and attacked him with a poker. Even after the arrival of the police, Gougain continued to strike Sweeney, who at this point was on the ground with a severe head injury. Gougain was taken into custody.

2 OCTOBER   **1852**   While a gentleman was walking along one of the city streets, a woman bumped into him, dropping a phial containing a dark mixture as she did so. Exclaiming, 'Dear me – my child's medicine!', the woman was reimbursed by the man for the cost of the supposed medicine. The gentleman, however, was told by a passer-by afterwards that he had seen the same trick carried out by the woman the day before.

3 OCTOBER   **1845**   About nine o'clock at night, a man was found lying in the Bridgegate in an 'insensible condition'. Being seemingly under the influence of alcohol, the man was taken to the police office in a hurley, and had been expected to sleep off the effects of this excess. However, the next day when he remained in the same condition, medical aid was obtained. Despite this, the man died the following day, and, on examination, it was found he died from a severe fracture of the skull, not alcohol consumption. The circumstances surrounding his injury were never established.

4 OCTOBER   **1822**   A woman was apprehended in Wigton following the discovery of the body of a female infant in a field on the outskirts of the city. The woman later confessed that the child was hers and that she had strangled her. It appeared that the woman was a servant and the child had been illegitimate. It was reported that she had 'become prey to all the agonies of mental torture from the moment she perpetrated the barbarous deed'.

5 OCTOBER   **1849**   It was reported at the police office that James Cairnie, a spirit dealer from New Wynd, along with his two nieces, had been severely injured by the explosion of a gun. Cairnie had been amusing

A young worker in a
Victorian cotton mill.

himself by shooting through a small window in the house, and one
of the nieces, Agnes Cairnie, had been loading the gun for him.
On the last occasion, however, she had put too much powder into
it, and on attempting to fire it, the piece burst and severely injured
James Cairnie's arms and hands. The two girls were also hurt by the
explosion, and with their clothes having caught fire, they were also
badly burned.

6 OCTOBER   **1820**   Around this time, a series of brutal attacks had been carried
out on cotton spinners, both male and female, who were believed to
have taken the jobs of others who had been dismissed for either bad
conduct or for seeking better conditions. The pay and conditions at
this time for cotton spinners had been particularly bad and many
had campaigned for better treatment. Employers, however, knowing
that there was a shortage of work for people, could always find those
willing to work for whatever pay was being offered, however small the
amount. One young man, who had been employed in Messrs Robert
Humphrey & Co.'s mill, and had previously worked for reduced rates,
was accosted by a man who, after giving him abuse, proceeded to
throw a quantity of vitriol in his face. Vitriol was a strong mineral
acid, now better known as sulphuric acid.

7 OCTOBER   **1893**   Michael Grove, a returned convict who was arrested the day
before, made a 'desperate attempt to gain freedom' at the Eastern
Police Court, by jumping through one of the glass windows into the
street. Falling a distance of twenty or thirty feet, Grove sustained a
fracture of the leg and other serious injuries. He was taken to the
Infirmary in a critical condition.

8 OCTOBER   **1845**   Soldier, Michael McGrath of the 77th Regiment, put an end to his life by hanging himself. Having acted as an officer's servant, McGrath was a married man who lived with his wife and two children in lodgings in the vicinity of the barracks. McGrath, who had been drinking, ended up having an altercation with his wife. Shortly afterwards, a comrade of his came knocking at the door and the voice of one of the children within answered, 'the door is barred and daddy is hanging himself.' The door was instantly broken open, but instead of cutting McGrath down, the man ran to the barracks for assistance, during which time McGrath had died.

9 OCTOBER   **1853**   In Great City Road, Alexander Anderson, a spirit dealer, engaged in some petty argument with his wife, who had recently given birth to their child. Anderson, taking exception to his wife's comments on his conduct, kicked her in the abdomen, causing an internal haemorrhage. Realising that his temper had resulted in a serious injury, he ran for medical aid, but the nature of the injury rendered help useless. Mrs Anderson only had time to declare that it was her husband who had assaulted her before she died. Anderson was taken into custody.

10 OCTOBER   **1845**   Mrs Watson, who had been in service at Braehead House, had the privilege of supplying herself with pot herbs from the garden. However, it became suspected that she had also been taking some of the 'superior kinds of fruit', and she was dismissed. The indignity of this was said to have 'affected her strongly' and she became depressed and 'somewhat disordered in mind'. After an investigation into the matter though, Mrs Watson was cleared of all blame. Unfortunately this did not help her mental state, and one morning she was found lying on the floor with a razor close at hand, dying in a pool of blood. After her funeral, however, the authorities decided to have her body disinterred for the purpose of examination, with the result that her husband was committed to jail on suspicion of murder.

11 OCTOBER   **1850**   In a case of suspected child murder, a woman was taken into custody. The woman, named Sutherland, a servant to a family in the Gorbals, proposed to get a pennyworth of something she called 'poppy' to administer to one of the family's children who was sick.

Not being aware of what 'poppy' was, the lady of the house agreed and gave Sutherland the money, with which she purchased laudanum. The drug was then sweetened with sugar and given to the child, who was two months old, without the knowledge of the mother. The child died later that evening and Sutherland was arrested in the Night Asylum, where she had gone to stay after the incident.

12 OCTOBER   1850   Early in the morning, whilst several people were on their way to work, they caught sight of a 'labouring man' who was lying sound asleep on a quantity of 'slag' which had been thrown out from Mr Dixon's Iron Works. One of the people went forward to rouse the man, but it was found that he was dead. It was thought that having lay down on the slag, the sulphurous fumes which it emitted had suffocated him. These Iron Works had been the first to be established in Glasgow, and the light from the blast furnace fires lit up the Glasgow skyline both day and night.

13 OCTOBER   1856   Outside a house in Gallowgate, a large crowd had assembled after a fire was discovered. Among the crowd were a number of

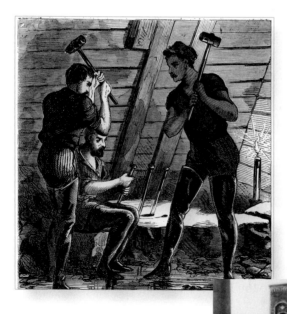

Right: Dixon's No. 5 Coal Pit, courtesy of Transport Scotland.

thieves and pickpockets, two of which were James Simpson and James Henderson. During the commotion, an old weaver named William Alison who had been seeing some of his friends, was passing up High Street. Thinking he was an easy target, Simpson and Henderson followed him, and, managing to get him into a close, seized him by the throat, knocked him down and attempted to rob him. Fortunately Alison's cries brought the assistance of the police, but on their arrival Simpson and Henderson pretended that they had been the ones assaulted by the old weaver. Seeing through this, the police took them into custody and they were sent to prison for sixty days with hard labour.

14 OCTOBER

1822 The newspapers on this date featured the public whipping of William Storrier and John Miller who were recently convicted for rape. It was reported that about 10,000 spectators had assembled on the streets, with most of the windows also crowded with people watching. The culprits backs were bared and a cord was run round their wrists and fastened to the cart, then they were drawn through the city streets, stopping thirteen times and receiving thirteen lashes each time. Storrier was said to have seemed indifferent, but Miller was apparently 'greatly affected' by the punishment. After this they received the next part of their sentence, which was fourteen years' transportation.

15 OCTOBER

1806 Adam Cox, a labourer living in the Calton district of the city who was originally from Ireland, was apprehended and lodged in Glasgow Jail on suspicion of drowning his own child. The body of the child had been found in a clay pit in Tradeston. Cox was later convicted of the crime at the Glasgow Circuit Court and sentenced to death. After the execution, Cox's body was given to the Professor of Anatomy for dissection, which was common practice at the time, due to the shortage of bodies for medical students to practice their skills on. He was said to have 'fully acknowledged his guilt of the crime' whilst he was on the scaffold. Cox had another three children, who were admitted to the Town's Hospital after his death.

16 OCTOBER

1845 During a fire which had taken place in a wood yard in the Gorbals, a poor woman who had been alarmed by the close proximity of the flames to her house, was struggling with a child in her arms to exit the building. A thief, seeing her distressed circumstances, took

THE DEATH SENTENCE.

A newspaper headline from around the time of McKay's execution.

advantage of the situation by ripping open the side of her gown and taking her money from her pocket.

17 OCTOBER **1927** A man appeared at the Central Police Court on this date, charged with murder. James McKay, looking 'dejected and dazed' was accused of having murdered his mother, Agnes Arbuckle, at 213 Main Street, South Side, Glasgow. After the mutilated remains of Mrs Arbuckle had been identified by McKay's wife, detectives had made a search of the house and taken possession of a small saw and some other incriminating items. McKay was the only surviving son of the victim, his two brothers having lost their lives during the First World War. It appeared that McKay had been 'a considerable alcoholic', whose excessive drinking had led to him get into arrears with his rent, and although his mother had helped him by giving him money, he had spent it on drink. During the course of a quarrel between them, McKay had slashed his mother on the face and neck, killing her, and then spent around two hours dismembering her body. It was reported that after the murder, he had also gone around trying to sell her false teeth. At his trial, McKay's plea of temporary insanity was not upheld, as it had been proven that he had attempted to forge his mother's signature on several documents in an attempt to steal her savings. Being found guilty, the sentence of death was passed on McKay, who turned to his wife, waved his cap and said 'cheer up'.

18 OCTOBER **1850** John Savage, described as a 'drunken blackguard', was sentenced to sixty days' imprisonment in the Bridewell, after brutally assaulting, striking and kicking in the stomach a woman named Mary O'Brien, a lodger in the same house in New Vennel. Mary O'Brien's internal injuries were so severe that it was thought she might die through the loss of blood.

19 OCTOBER **1849** Thomas Cufney, a shoemaker in Main Street, was brought before the Southern District Police Court, charged with an unprovoked assault on his wife and father-in-law. For a considerable time, Cufney had 'persisted in wandering about idle' and this had not been the first time he had appeared in court for such domestic assaults. The charge being found proven, he was sentenced to sixty days' imprisonment.

20 OCTOBER   **1851**   At about one o'clock in the afternoon, an explosion of gas took place in a house in Holm Street, causing serious injury to two men. After a strong smell of gas had been noticed, two officers of the Old Gas Company had been instructed to attend at the house to make the necessary examination and repairs. On arriving at the house, they found the leak to be coming from an underground cellar, where they proceeded with a lighted candle. The door to the cellar was no sooner opened when a loud explosion took place, shaking the whole building. Part of the pavement was torn up in the blast and the two men were so burned on the face and head, it was thought they would be disfigured for life.

21 OCTOBER   **1844**   Another gas explosion took place on this date, in Pearson's land, adjoining the railway station in Bridge Street. The gas had been escaping in one of the rooms during the course of the day, and that night when a servant girl entered with a candle, the explosion instantly took place. The girl was knocked down by the blast, which sounded to the people in the tenement and at the railway station like 'a discharge of artillery'. The room door was smashed to pieces and the window was blown out, with several panes of glass also broken in the adjoining windows.

22 OCTOBER   **1847**   A case of alleged poisoning came under the attention of the Glasgow Police, believed to have been carried out under 'much cool deliberation and atrocity'. A man named Keenan, a labourer living in Hunter Street, had died a few days previously under suspicious circumstances, and the criminal officer Clark proceeded to the house to make inquiries. As a result of these inquiries, Keenan's wife was taken into custody on a charge of murder.

On the day he died, Keenan had been drinking and it appeared that whilst he was drunk a quantity of laudanum had been administered to him. It also emerged that Mrs Keenan had sent out for two pennyworths of laudanum, which together with the information that the Keenan's marriage was not a happy one, led to suspicion falling on her. Mrs Keenan pleaded not guilty to the charge and the case went to trial. A young girl named Catherine Brogan gave evidence that she had been sent by the woman to purchase the laudanum, and on the day of the incident she had seen Mrs Keenan mix the laudanum in a jug of porter and give it to her husband. Catherine also told the court that she had been frequently sent out by Mrs Keenan for whisky in the afternoons, of which Mr Keenan drank large amounts. The surgeons who had examined the body confirmed that in their opinion, death had been caused by opium from the laudanum. However, they also admitted that the appearance of opium in a dead body could look very similar to excessive alcohol consumption. The jury, after hearing the evidence, returned a verdict of 'not proven' and Mrs Keenan was discharged from the bar.

23 OCTOBER

1938 Having been arrested at the Royal Infirmary following the death of his wife, William Morrison, alias Christie, appeared at the Southern Police Court on a charge of murder. The charge was that Morrison had struck his wife on the face and body and knocked her to the ground, whereby she received injuries that resulted in her death. Witnesses had seen Morrison's wife fall to the ground at the junction of West Street and Morrison Street late at night, and realising that she had head injuries, they summoned an 'ambulance wagon'. She was taken to the Royal Infirmary, but was found to be dead on arrival.

24 OCTOBER

1850 Early in the morning, a man who gave his name as Thomas Walker, reported at the Gorbals Police Office that he had been attacked about ten o'clock the previous night. Walker told police that while he was in Rutherglen Loan, three men accosted him and attempted to take his watch and money, and one of the men had tried to throw something around his neck while he was on the ground. Walker, however, who had a whip in his hand, managed to strike the man in the face at which point he let go of his grip and the ran off along with the other two assailants.

25 OCTOBER

1850 In the Old Vennel an 'atrocious assault' was committed on Mrs Collins, 'a poor widow woman', by her son. Whilst she was sitting at her fireside about six o'clock in the evening, her son Philip entered the house in a state of intoxication, and, without any provocation, struck her a violent blow in the face, which cut open her left temple, causing blood to flow from the wound. On asking why he was doing this, Mrs Collins was again attacked by Philip, who hit her several times and kicked her violently on several parts of her body. Managing to get away from him, she reached the street and attempted to take shelter in a neighbour's house. However, Philip chased after his poor mother and picking up a knife from the neighbour's table, threatened to stab her in the heart. The neighbour tried to persuade him to give up the knife, but her request was only met with violence. By this time, however, a large crowd had assembled in the street and other neighbours assisted in taking Philip Collins into custody. In the Police Court he was sentenced to sixty days' imprisonment.

26 OCTOBER

1857 Duncan McGregor was charged at the Western Police Court with having assaulted his housekeeper, Margaret Reid. McGregor, a widower who lived in Bothwell Street, had come home on the night of the incident under the influence of alcohol. An altercation then ensued between him and Margaret Reid, which ended in McGregor knocking her down, kicking her, threatening to take her life and stabbing her in the forehead with a pair of scissors. A number of neighbours gave evidence as to the 'annoyance and disturbance' they had been subjected to by the violent conduct of McGregor. He was fined £2, 2s.

27 OCTOBER

1881 A case of 'murder by a lunatic' was heard in the Glasgow Circuit Court. John Black, a thirty-year-old man, was charged with having murdered a warder in the Govan Combination Poorhouse, by striking him on the head with a spade. A special defence was lodged in order to bar the trial on the grounds of the prisoner's insanity. The medical superintendent of the Glasgow District Asylum told the court he had attended Black, who was suffering from 'hallucinations of hearing' and that 'persons suffering that way' were among the 'most dangerous class of lunatics'. The medical officer in the 'lunatic asylum' at Govan also testified to the insane condition of the prisoner, at which point the court case was deserted and Black was ordered to be confined indefinitely.

28 OCTOBER

1882 A fire 'of a very destructive character' occurred in the Bridgeton district of Glasgow. A large cotton spinning mill was discovered to be on fire shortly after the employees left the building. The preparing department, a building over 200 feet in length and five storeys high, was 'enveloped in flames', causing damages of

£20,000 and resulting in the loss of 400 people's jobs, during a time of already high unemployment.

29 OCTOBER 1852 The report of a murder appeared in the newspapers on this day. On a previous morning, a weaver named Andrews, who had been drinking, proceeded to abuse his wife on returning home. On hearing this, an old man named McNee who lived in the same tenement, entered the house and tried to intervene. Andrews, in his angry state, turned upon McNee and dealt him such severe blows as to knock him to the floor, rendering him unconscious. McNee died within a very short time. Realising the seriousness of what he had done, Andrews instantly fled the scene.

30 OCTOBER 1826 A forty-year-old 'apparently respectable' woman went into a shop of a respectable surgeon in the city and offered to sell him her healthy two-month-old child for the price of £7. Having the child with her, she began to strip off the infant's clothes, stating that she wanted to retain them after the sale. The horrified surgeon was even more astounded when she additionally offered to sell him her thirteen-year-old son, suggesting he could 'do what he liked with him'. Having been taken to the police office, it was established that she had been separated from her husband for some time. It was thought that the woman must have been 'deranged'.

31 OCTOBER 1851 Whilst an omnibus was passing Paisley Road, opposite Kinning Park, the front horse suddenly stopped. The guard in an attempt to get the horse moving again, took hold of it by the head; however, in doing so the forefinger of his left hand became entangled in a chain connected with the collar and was ripped off at the second joint.

NOVEMBER

Jamaica Bridge, Glasgow.

A newspaper headline
from around the time
of Stewart and Kelly's
execution.

EXECUTION.

1 NOVEMBER

1826 Two men convicted of two separate robberies were executed on this date. Andrew Stewart had knocked down a 'foreign' man in the Gallowgate, in order that his associates could steal the man's gold watch, chain, key and two £1 notes. These items had later been shared amongst them. Stewart, although admitting to knocking the man down, strenuously denied that he had done so with the intention of robbing him. He had been a weaver by trade, and it was reported that at one time he had 'led a life of vice, wickedness and debauchery'.

Edward Kelly had robbed an old man in Bridgegate Street, stealing £108 from him. Kelly had been convicted along with another man named White, who was not facing the death penalty due to it being his first offence. Kelly's life had been described as 'one of crime and wickedness' and he had spent time in the Bridewell on twelve previous occasions.

A few minutes after eight o'clock, the magistrates entered the hall and the prisoners were brought up. Stewart came first, accompanied by the Revd Mr Marshall, and Kelly followed, accompanied by the Revd Mr Scott and the Revd Mr Murdoch.

They remained only a short time in the hall, where they partook of a glass of wine each, which was a customary practice before execution, to steady the condemned person's nerves. The procession then moved towards the scaffold, on ascending it, Stewart addressed the assembled crowd of spectators, saying in an emphatic tone, 'I have a few words to say to you all – beware of drunkenness – obey your parents – and do not profane the Sabbath day; for these are the crimes that have brought me to this deplorable condition. I bid you all a long farewell.' When the preparations for the executions were complete, the two men held hands and spent a few moments in prayer, before Stewart gave the signal and the drop fell. It was reported that Stewart died fairly quickly, but Kelly convulsed and 'suffered long'. Stewart's mother had been in the crowd and was seen to be in prayer during the proceedings and had given a loud shriek when the drop fell.

2 NOVEMBER

1857 At an office premises in St Vincent Street, a strong smell of gas had been noticed during the morning. The office clerk,

Argyle Street; on the corner between Argyle Street and Dunlop Street was situated the Buck's Head Hotel.

Mr Gordon, ascended a ladder with a light to examine the gasolier. On approaching the ceiling of the room, however, the light came into contact with a large quantity of gas which had been accumulating, and, as expected, a serious explosion took place. Both the clerk and Mr Anderson, the owner of the premises, were severely burned by the explosion, which had such a tremendous force that, after shattering the window, it blew down a building which was in the middle of construction at the back of the property. Glass fragments from the window were also blown right across the street.

3 NOVEMBER   **1849**   During the morning, a gentleman who was staying at the Buck's Head Hotel, committed suicide under 'somewhat melancholy circumstances'. It appeared that in the afternoon of the previous day he had been exhibiting symptoms of '*delirium tremens*' and a friend had been keeping an eye on his condition. However, on the morning in question, the friend left him for a few minutes, as he had seemed to be asleep in bed, but on his return had found the room empty and the window open. On searching the yard below, the man was discovered lying on the ground, almost dead. Two doctors came to assist, but his injuries were such that he died a short time later. The Buck's Head Hotel, a grand building on the corner of Arglye Street and Dunlop Street, had been one of Glasgow's most popular hotels in the Victorian era. The building was demolished in 1862 and replaced by the Buck's Head Buildings which stand today.

4 NOVEMBER **1850** At the station of the Caledonian Railway in Buchanan Street, an accident occurred involving a labourer named Cornelius Foy. Foy had been cleaning the rails within the station when a number of empty wagons were suddenly set in motion, and before he had time to get out of the way, they knocked him down and ran right over his body. Foy's left leg was almost severed from his body and he had extensive severe bruising throughout. He was taken from the station to the Infirmary.

5 NOVEMBER **1890** A murder 'of a shocking character' was committed late at night in the north of the city. At number 19 Rodney Street, which was a narrow, dark lane leading from Possil Road, a wedding feast had been in full swing. The bride had been Miss Margaret Powell, daughter of a pattern maker, and the bridegroom was a young Italian man named Laurence Lonni, an ice-cream and confectionary seller. The marriage had become well known within the Italian community in the neighbourhood and a number of people had turned up to the feast uninvited. Among them was a youth named Marco, who had been asked to leave, which he did, but had then returned just before midnight with an associate named Palembo. Both were reluctantly admitted, but soon afterwards they were asked to leave again. The two men, along with a number of other men attending the party then ended up in a quarrel in the street, which resulted in two ice-cream vendors, Andro Luciano and Michal Gizzie, being stabbed. Luciano, who had been stabbed in the chest, died almost immediately. The cries of the women present attracted the attention of the police, who arrested Marco.

6 NOVEMBER **1846** Robert Baird, a young man employed at an iron works, lost his footing and fell on a red-hot rail behind him whilst drawing a heavy rail from the rolls. In an effort to remove himself from the burning bar, however, he managed to throw himself upon the circular saw, which was in full operation. Baird was 'sawn and torn in such a shocking manner', that onlookers ran from the scene in terror.

7 NOVEMBER **1818** On this date, newspapers reported the execution of Mathew Clydesdale for murder. Clydesdale had been found guilty at the Glasgow Circuit Court, of the murder of an old man named Alexander Love with a pickaxe. The murder was thought to have been 'perpetrated wantonly' whilst Clydesdale had been in a state of intoxication. On the

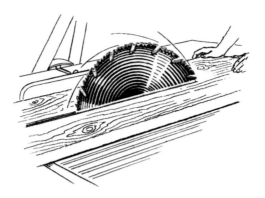

A drawing of a circular saw.

day of execution, he faced the scaffold alongside another man, who had been convicted of a separate crime. After the usual prayers, the two men proceeded to the scaffold, with Clydesdale seeming indifferent to his fate. An immense crowd had assembled to watch the execution, which took place at five minutes past three o'clock in the afternoon, when Clydesdale was said to have died quickly after the drop fell.

After hanging for nearly an hour, the bodies were cut down and Clydesdale's was put into a coffin and then onto a cart to be transported to the Professor of Anatomy for dissection. The dissection, however, took on a more unusual form than other such procedures. On arrival at the college, the body proceeded with the throng of students to the lecture hall, which was packed with students and 'the respectable citizens of Glasgow'. The body was handed over to Dr Andrew Ure of the chemistry class, who was assisted by Professor Jeffrey, and placed in an armchair facing the audience. Dr Ure had been seeking to prove that by stimulating the phrenic nerve, life could be restored in cases such as hanging or suffocation.

A light air tube connected with a galvanic battery was placed in one of Clydesdale's nostrils and the bellows began to blow, inflating his chest. The other nostril was similarly treated, and soon Clydesdale's eyes opened, his limbs moved, his head also moved appearing as if he

Dr Andrew Ure.

was looking around, and the corpse rose upright on its feet. Some of the students screamed, others fainted and many applauded. To put an end to the experiment, Professor Jeffrey took out his lancet and plunged it into the jugular vein of the dead man, who instantly fell on the floor. This spectacular display was thought to have influenced Mary Shelley when writing her novel, *Frankenstein*.

8 NOVEMBER   **1884**   On the corner of Gallowgate Street and Watson Street, the Star Theatre was the scene of a terrible tragedy in which fifteen people died. The theatre had been an entertainment venue aimed at the working class and had always been very well attended. Shortly after the doors had been opened on the fateful evening, the house was filled and the performance commenced. Everything was going smoothly until a few minutes after nine o'clock when, suddenly, panic broke out. The Eugene Family, a troupe of acrobats, had appeared on the stage and ascended the ladder to the several trapezes which were suspended from the roof. While the youngest of the Eugenes was preparing for his leap from one of the bars, however, a man in the dress circle who was drunk, shouted, 'fire, fire!' In an instant, the whole audience was panic stricken and rushed towards the doors. A stampede ensued, with people trampling over those who had fallen, all the while thinking there was a fire somewhere in the building, which of course, there was not. Once the majority of the audience had left he building, the full extent of the disaster was realised. Every cab passing the theatre at the time was used to carry the dead and wounded to the infirmary. James Turner, the man who had given the alarm falsely, was arrested.

9 NOVEMBER   **1889**   In James Templeton and Co.'s carpet works, an accident occurred which was described as 'one of the most appalling that has taken place in the city for many years'. During a strong gale, a large addition to the premises which had been built, collapsed and crashed through an adjourning weaving shed. The incident occurred at quarter past five, whilst at least 140 girls were at work. Many were

Newspaper clipping of the tragedy at the Star Theatre.

PANIC IN A GLASGOW MUSIC HALL.
FIFTEEN PERSONS KILLED.

buried in the ruins. The fire brigade arrived and using an electric wire and incandescent lamp to provide light, a rescue party was put in place. The dead bodies were discovered near to what had been an entrance to the old building in which they had been working. The injured girls were taken to the Royal Infirmary in ambulance wagons. A crowd of relatives and friends of the workers assembled outside the building waiting eagerly to hear news of those missing. Some of the dead workers were said to be 'terribly disfigured' and one of the victims had been completely decapitated. The finishing shed of the mill was converted into a temporary mortuary into which relatives were admitted to identify the bodies. Thirty people in total had been killed in the tragedy.

10 NOVEMBER   **1848**   As one of the night constables was on duty at the High Street, he was accosted by a man who wished the watchman to accompany him up a close in search of a party that had stolen money from him. The watchman, however, distrusting the appearance of the individual, refused to go along with him. At this point the man brandished a large knife, stating that he would either take his own life or that of the some other person. On seeing the knife, the watchman attempted to disarm him, but ended up receiving a cut to the hand which nearly severed one of his fingers. Fortunately another constable arrived at this moment and helped get the knife out of the man's grasp. He was taken into custody and received a sentence of sixty days' imprisonment in the Police Court.

11 NOVEMBER   **1844**   As two carters from Anderston, 'in a state of intoxication' and in charge of two horses and carts, were proceeding along the road, one of them ran forward and struck the other's horse, which sprang forward and the tram of the cart came into contact with a woman who was passing at the time. The woman was knocked to the ground, sustained serious injuries to the head and had one of her arms broken. She was taken to the Royal Infirmary, whilst the men were apprehended and taken into custody.

12 NOVEMBER   **1852**   James Hamilton from St Andrew's Street, described as 'a blackguard', was charged in the Central Police Court with having been drunk and disorderly within his mother's shop, and of having assaulted her. Hamilton was also charged with threatening to take his mother's life and with 'being in the practice of conducting himself in a similar manner'. The charges were found proven and Hamilton was fined three guineas.

13 NOVEMBER   **1820**   A forty-year-old man who had been 'in a very unsettled state of mind', left his house despite his aged parents urging him to remain there, and threw himself into the Clyde. The man was drowned before his mother, who followed him 'as fast as her strength would permit, could reach him. Entering the water, she reached the spot where her son was, but it was too late to save his life.

14 NOVEMBER   **1845**   Two soldiers and three 'working men' were tried before the sitting magistrate of the Glasgow Police Court for being involved in a serious riot in High Street on the previous Saturday evening. From the evidence it appeared that they were 'the worse of liquor' at the time, and they had proceeded to threaten a spirit dealer and his wife in their own shop. Having resisted arrest, they had been rescued by a mob, but afterwards the police caught up with them again. At this point a riot broke out involving brick bats flying in all directions and some of the policemen sustained serious injuries. In court the offence was found proven against three of the men and one of the soldiers, a sergeant, was fined one guinea. The other soldier, a private, was fined half a guinea; as was one of the working men.

15 NOVEMBER   **1821**   A young girl who was about to get married, but unable to find the money to purchase a wedding outfit, decided to submit to the operation of having five front teeth removed in order to obtain money for the clothes. She was paid five guineas. At this time it was thought that teeth could be 'implanted' into the mouths of those who had lost teeth. It was not uncommon for the poor to sell their teeth for money, particularly as the poorer people had better teeth that the rich, as they could not afford sweet treats.

16 NOVEMBER   **1854**   A woman named Margaret Inglis was convicted at the Southern Police Court of embezzling a large quantity of clothing, bed clothes and other household articles, which had been the property of the Govan Parochial authorities. It appeared that she had three boys who had been inmates of the poorhouse, and the Board had encouraged her to get them sent out to trades and to take them home with herself. To enable her to do so they supplied the boys with sufficient clothing

Nineteenth-century
dentistry apparatus.

and gave her bed clothes and other articles for this purpose. However she immediately sold them to a broker in the High Street and spent the proceeds. Inglis was sentenced to sixty days in prison.

17 NOVEMBER   **1853**   A police constable was in Miller Street when he discovered a man lying in a state of unconsciousness upon the pavement 'through the effects of intoxicating liquor'. The man was taken to the Central Police Office where he sobered up and told the officers he was a manufacturer from Alva, in Clackmannanshire, who had been 'a little upon the spree'. During the course of the night however, the man stated that he had become very thirsty and asked for something to drink. Having been supplied with this drink, he repaid the officer attending him by pitching the tin can containing the water at the officer's head, cutting him. For this offence, as well as being 'drunk and unable', the manufacturer was fined one guinea.

18 NOVEMBER   **1853**   Hugh Fury, an Irish labourer, whilst 'in a state of intoxication', got into a quarrel within a spirit shop with an elderly man named

The former Central Police Office today, which later became Glasgow District Court but is now unused.

Alexander Brown. Fury boasted that he was 'the brightest Orangeman in the house', to which Brown responded by saying that he was 'no party man' but that he was a Freemason. Fury, becoming noticeably angry, stated that a Freemason had killed his father, and then proceeded to strike Brown, knocking him to the ground. Fury was fined one guinea at the Western Police Court.

19 NOVEMBER   1891   In the Parkhead area, a forty-three-year-old woman named Catherine Marshall was standing at the mouth of a close at 287 Old Edinburgh Road. She had been standing there talking to a labourer named William Geddes, when she started to sing, 'Who will hold the horses, whoa, whoa, whoa'. A young man named Joseph Ketchin, a fireman who lived in Auburn Place, came up at that moment and enquired as to the whereabouts of a man he was looking for. Catherine told him that she didn't know the man and resumed her singing, when suddenly, and without warning, Ketchin drew a revolver from his pocket and shot her in the eye, shouting, 'That is "whoa" to you!' The bullet passed through Catherine's skull and she dropped down dead. At Ketchin's trial, the jury returned a verdict of culpable homicide and he was sentenced to three months' imprisonment.

of drowning. Those in need of assistance tended to consist of people who were trying to cross the river or those who had fallen off ships. The society had been a necessary introduction as at this time it was incredibly difficult to get members of the public to help people needing assistance in the water. This was due to the fact that jumping into the river was a common method of suicide and at this time, with attempting suicide being a criminal act, any member of the public going to assist a person in difficulty was in danger of being thought of as an accessory to the crime. Due to the ever-demanding need for rescuers, the Glasgow Humane Society decided in 1859 to put a full-time officer in place for carrying out rescues and recovering the bodies of those who had drowned. Prior to this the Humane Society, like many others, had set up a system of rewarding rescuers with medals and certificates in order to entice people to help.

27 NOVEMBER **1848** At about half past ten o'clock in the evening, the residents of the High Street were considerably alarmed by a man named Wood. Wood, a painter who lived in the area, had got hold of an old sword with which he assaulted his sister, inflicting a severe wound. Another woman who was unfortunate enough to come within his reach at the time, was also slashed with the sword, as was a policeman who attempted to take him into custody. It was thought that Wood was either suffering from '*delirium tremens* or insanity'. He was finally overpowered when more police constables arrived, and was taken to the police office.

28 NOVEMBER **1845** At about six o'clock in the evening, an infant wrapped in a tartan shawl was found lying in a doorway of a close at 142 George Street. The person who left the child there was not found, despite the matter being investigated. Newspapers at the time commented that 'the exposure of infants in this way' had been 'much less frequent than it was two or three years ago'.

29 NOVEMBER **1858** The Revd John McKenzie, a licensed preacher and a missionary, was charged with 'a piece of scandalous and outrageous conduct'. Revd McKenzie had previously complained to the police about an annoyance which he alleged was caused by one of his neighbours. The officers inquired into the matter and on finding that there were no grounds for complaint, decided not to interfere and went on their way. However, half an later the reverend again went to the police office, this time with a drawn sword in his hand, threatening to stab the officers if they would not apprehend his neighbour. The two officers accompanied by their sergeant, went with him to his own house and tried to persuade him to stop his behaviour. Enraged by this, Revd McKenzie chased the officers down the stairs with the sword and stabbed the sergeant in the forehead with it. It was reported that the reverend was 'much the worse of liquor' at the time.

30 NOVEMBER **1849** A woman with two infants, thought to be around eight years old, was admitted to the Night Asylum. However, the next morning it was found that both children had died during the course of the night with the cause of death being unapparent. Dr Watson, the medical officer of the asylum, made an immediate examination of the bodies, but no marks of violence were found. The bodies were interred at the expense of the town's hospital and no further inquiry was made into the matter.

DECEMBER

Charing Cross in 1900.

1 DECEMBER **1848** At around half past six in the evening, a carter named Jack heard a loud splash whilst walking along the canal, followed immediately by piercing screams. Jack ran forward and despite the low light, saw a woman struggling in the water. He managed, after some difficulty, to drag the woman to the bank. In an 'exhausted condition', she was taken to the Gorbals Police Office where she told the police what had happened. It appeared that whilst she was walking along by the canal, a labourer came up to her and started a conversation. He had offered to carry the bundle she had in her arms, which consisted of some bed clothes. However, on taking up the man's seemingly kind offer, he gave her a sudden push into the water and ran off.

2 DECEMBER **1822** Whilst a young man and woman were walking along the road on the outskirts of the city early in the evening, they were attacked by three men. The man received 'a stroke with a bludgeon', upon which he ran to the other side of the road and shouted, 'murder! He was followed, however, and knocked down, at which time his watch was stolen. The young woman was also knocked down, but a carriage coming along the road at the time fortunately made the robbers run off and put an end to the assault.

3 DECEMBER **1849** Grace Miller, described as 'a poor woman', was found at the door of the Renfield Street Free Church, near to death. It appeared that her husband, Thomas Miller, had been an inmate of the Clyde Street Hospital for some weeks, and as Mrs Miller had no other means of support, she had resorted to selling apples on the streets to earn

Looking westwards
down the Broomielaw.
(Courtesy of Ben
Brooksbank)

some money. Whilst in Broomielaw with a basket of fruit, she had sat down complaining of exhaustion. Soon afterwards she began to cough and grew very ill. Mrs Miller died before she could be helped from the spot where she had been found and was taken to the Central Police Office, where her body was examined. It was the opinion of the police surgeon that she had died from the effects of asthma, whilst in a weak condition through lack of food.

4 DECEMBER **1846** Early in the afternoon, a 'melancholy and fatal accident' happened at a former starching works, situated at the back of the Gorbals Foundry. A labourer was engaged in excavating near the foot of a brick wall when, due to too much loose sand having been dug out near the foundation of the wall, it suddenly gave way and fell, bringing down with it the flooring above as well as part of the roofing. The labourer became buried in the rubble and work was immediately commenced to remove him from the mass of materials which had fallen. After about two hours of exertion, the, sadly deceased, body of the man was reached – a look of agony still present on his face.

5 DECEMBER **1848** At Anderston Police Court, a woman named McGowan, described as 'a miserable-looking female', was charged with permitting her children, a boy and girl aged six and eight years old respectively, to go around the streets begging. The children, along with their mother, had been brought before the magistrate on a previous occasion, at which time she had promised to allow them to remain in the Industrial School. However, it seemed that they had not

A Victorian prison cell
with oakum on the
table ready to be picked.
(Courtesy of Dave
Hitchbourne)

be present at the school for long when the woman had taken them
away and sent them once more to the streets. She was sentenced to
twenty days' imprisonment.

6 DECEMBER   1852   At the Southern District Police Court, Elizabeth Kelly, who
had been remanded from the previous day, was charged with having,
'while in a state of intoxication, violently assaulted and injured
her father', described as 'an old grey headed man'. The offence
having been found proven, and as she had been convicted of the
same 'unnatural crime' before, Kelly was sentenced to sixty days'
imprisonment with hard labour. Hard labour in prisons, particularly

for women, typically consisted of picking oakum. This was tedious work, involving untwisting and unpicking old hemp rope until it was reduced to individual fibres, which could be sold on.

7 DECEMBER **1858** Williamina McGonagall, a young woman described as 'having a very bad temper', was charged with having, whilst in a hostel for girls at Athol House, assaulted a girl by brandishing a knife and with placing a quantity of picric acid in a kettle with the intention of injuring the matron and other staff members. McGonagall pleaded not guilty. However, after evidence had been heard, the sheriff found the charge involving the knife proven, but the charge involving the poison not proven. As the sheriff considered the crime of brandishing a knife to be 'of a trivial nature', McGonagall was allowed to go after being given a warning to control her temper.

8 DECEMBER **1888** John McMillan, described as 'a respectable looking man', appeared in court to answer a charge of assault upon his wife. McMillan denied the assault which was said to have taken place in the couple's house in Tylefield Street, where Mrs McMillan, who was 'in an advanced state of pregnancy' had been struck with a coat and hat, kicked, seized by the hair, pulled out of bed. McMillan was also accused of attempting to stab her with a knife. Evidence was given by Mrs McMillan, her son and a neighbour to the effect that she had been in bed when her husband had come home 'the worse for drink'. After he had finished his supper, McMillan had asked her to get up and make more for him, which she had refused to do. McMillan responded by smashing one of the dishes and throwing a piece of the broken dish at her, which missed Mrs McMillan but cut her son. McMillan then pulled her out of the bed by the hair, kicked her, threatened to 'knock out her brains', and standing over her with a knife, said he would 'do Jack the Ripper' with her, a reference of course to the murders which were being carried out in London at the time. The jury unanimously found him guilty, and as there were no less than eight previous convictions against him, several of which being for assaults on his wife, he was sentenced to six months' imprisonment.

9 DECEMBER **1853** At about nine o'clock at night, whilst a young man was passing through Dunlop Street, he was invited by a female to speak with her in an entry there. The man, described as 'a simpleton', had no sooner entered the close into which the woman was enticing him when he was seized by the throat by a man. The man, working together with the woman, held him so tightly round the neck that he could not breathe and robbed him of a silver watch. The thief was pursued after some other young men who had witnessed the goings-on, raised the alarm. He was apprehended whilst throwing away the watch in an attempt to avoid identification.

10 DECEMBER 1857 Edward Finlay, otherwise known as 'Penny-a-Yard', was charged at the Central Police Court with being drunk and disorderly, and of violently resisting the two constables who were taking him into custody. For these offences, Finlay was sentenced to thirty days' imprisonment. The *Glasgow Herald* newspaper reported that, 'This worthless old fellow is continually giving trouble to the police by his drunkenness and misconduct, and yet he is encouraged to remain in Glasgow as a pest, by the mistaken charity of his street patrons.'

11 DECEMBER 1848 Mr Scott, an inspector of the poor in the Barony Parish, having reason to believe that a man named Rennie had been guilty of deserting his wife and children, went to his residence in Greenvale Street for the purpose of apprehending him. However, on being made aware of the reason for the inspector's visit, Rennie not only refused to go along with him to the police office, but struck the inspector several times with his fists, only stopping when some of the neighbours intervened. At the Police Court, Rennie was found guilty of the charges and fined two guineas. Additionally, as there was a suspicion that his wife had been guilty of 'systematic imposition on the parochial authorities', she was detained for examination on the charge.

12 DECEMBER 1924 Father of five, Samuel Redmond, admitted in the Glasgow Sheriff Court, a serious assault upon his ten-year-old son. It appeared that Redmond's wife had died three years previously and he had been bringing up the children whose ages ranged from three to thirteen years, on his own. On the afternoon of the incident, when Redmond had returned home from work, he was told that the ten-year-old boy had stolen 1s from an older brother. Taking the boy into a bedroom, Redmond stripped the boy naked and thrashed him with a leather belt. The boy, who was bruised all over his body, said that after he had been thrashed, his father rubbed salt into the wounds, causing him excruciating pain. Two days later, when the boy had gone to the

Education Authority hostel for a meal, he was still unable to sit down. On staff there noticing that additionally, the boy could hardly stand up either, they took him to a medical clinic, where he was examined by two doctors, who sent him to the Sick Children's Hospital. Sheriff Blair, addressing Redmond, said 'If the law allowed me I would give you the cat', referring to a flogging with the cat-o'-nine-tails. Redmond was sentenced to six months' imprisonment with hard labour.

13 DECEMBER **1926** In the North Court, Margaret Nisbet was accused of attempting to murder her three young children, at her house in Bothwell Street, by cutting their throats with a razor. Nisbet pleaded not guilty with the special defence of insanity at the time of the crime. Eleven-year-old William Nisbet, was the first witness called. He told the court that Margaret Nesbit was his stepmother, and the three injured children: Alexander aged three, Edward aged two, and infant Mary, were his step siblings. At half past eight on the evening in question, whilst his father was out, William had been told by Margaret that he could go out, and when he returned the kitchen had been in darkness, but by the light of the fire he could see that his stepmother was in bed and the children were with her. Not realising that anything was wrong, William had gone into another room, and some time later he heard his father come in. The young boy then told the court that he heard his father exclaim, 'Oh dear,' at which point William ran into the kitchen to find his father tearing up cloth and placing it to the necks of the children and his wife. Mr Nisbet had lifted up the eldest child and William had realised that the child's throat was cut. When the police arrived they lifted up a note which was on the mantlepiece and a razor from the bed. The note said:

> Dear Willie, forgive me for this, as my head has been something awful these last two days. I cannot stand it any longer. I had to go to the pawn to try and get the rent, but I only lost my few shillings, so I will take the wee ones too. If you are put out you will only have to get a place for you and Willie.
> Your loving wife, Mary.

The police doctor told the court that the four injured persons had lost a lot of blood, but luckily the cuts had not been deep enough to cause serious injury. The jury after a brief absence, unanimously found Mrs Nisbet guilty of the crime, but insane when she committed it. She received the usual sentence of being detained during His Majesty's pleasure.

14 DECEMBER   **1883**   In the northern district of Glasgow, Galbraith MacPherson, described as 'a young person of means', shot an actress from London and then killed himself. The actress, Grace Hamilton, had been about to start playing the part of a fairy at the forthcoming pantomime in the Grand Theatre. She returned to her lodgings from a rehearsal at four o'clock in the morning, and had been asleep when MacPherson had called on her in the afternoon. Mrs Dean, the owner of the lodging house stated that MacPherson had been the one to book the room for her to stay in and had visited her frequently. On this particular day, he had gone to her room and shortly afterwards, Mrs Dean heard the sound of a pistol shot. She immediately went into the room and found MacPherson leaning over Grace and covering her face with the blankets. MacPherson told Mrs Dean that he had only been giving Grace a fright; however, Mrs Dean pulled the blankets off the young woman's face and saw that she was bleeding from her head.

The landlady ran from the room and MacPherson closed the door after her. The sound of another pistol shot was heard at this point, and Mrs Dean ran out to summon the police. On her return, along with two constables, she found both Grace Hamilton and Galbraith MacPherson dead. A letter was found on the desk, which MacPherson had written to his mother asking her to forgive him for what he had done. Jealousy was thought to be the motive for the crime.

15 DECEMBER   **1827**   James Glen, convicted in the High Court of Justiciary for the murder of his child, was executed in front of the Glasgow Jail. Glen, who had killed the child by throwing it into the canal, was said to have been 'truly penitent' for the crime he had committed. Having resigned himself to his fate, he had taken religious instruction in the lead up to his execution, and had stated he was 'under the influence of the devil' when he committed the crime. At about two o'clock,

A newspaper clipping of the execution of James Glen – murderer of his own child.

EXECUTION OF JAMES GLEN.

the magistrates entered the Court Hall, followed by Glen, who took a few sips from a glass of wine. Deeply engaged in prayer, he ascended the steps to the scaffold. The rope was adjusted, the signal given, then the drop fell. After struggling briefly, Glen died and his body was allowed to hang for forty-five minutes. As usual for the time, his body was taken to the Professor of Anatomy for dissection. It was noted, however, that the Professor had agreed that no Galvanic experiments would be carried out on the executed man, as had been the case with Mathew Clydesdale a few years earlier. News of this greatly disappointed the public, who were keen to see another such macabre display.

16 DECEMBER **1850** A dreadful accident occurred on this date in the Corporation Pumping Station at Dumbarton Road, Partick. Thomas Knox, a labourer employed at the station, had been going about his usual tasks, when he suddenly saw a human hand revolving on one of the shafts. Knox immediately raised the alarm and the machinery was stopped. It transpired that Joseph Alexander, employed as a greaser, had been drawn into the machinery and killed. His remains were taken to the police mortuary.

17 DECEMBER **1849** John Riley, accused of 'thimble rigging' and of being 'a rogue and vagabond' was apprehended, having been found at Shawlands cheating people passing along the road by the game of thimble and peas. Riley was described as being 'idle and a disorderly person without lawful calling or fixed place of residence'. This game was a well used con at this time, where people would bet money on guessing which thimble the pea was under. The object of the game was to win more money if you guessed correctly, but the game would of course be rigged in order that the people playing the game never won.

18 DECEMBER **1928** Middle-aged man, James Reid, appeared at the High Court of Glasgow, charged with murdering his wife. The charge against Reid was that in their house in Nicholas Street, he had stabbed his wife, Annie Reid, with a knife, causing her death. Mrs Reid, just prior to her death in the Royal Infirmary, had given a statement that her husband had been out during the day with his son and a friend named Docherty, and on his return in the evening, they started quarrelling. Her son, who had been in the house at the time, had gone out saying he was not coming back, at which point James Reid grabbed her throat and cut it. A neighbour, Mrs Murray, gave evidence of hearing Mrs Reid shouting for assistance, and on going to the house and forcing her way in, found the woman leaning against the wall with blood coming from her neck and blood on the floor. Mrs Murray stated that Reid had said to her, 'It is Docherty's razor I done it with', further stating, 'she took it out of me.' There had been rumours at the time that Docherty and Mrs Reid had been having a relationship, which James Reid had become aware of. After hearing all the evidence, the jury found Reid guilty and he was sentenced to death.

19 DECEMBER 1851 At the Central Police Court, a woman named Mason was tried before the magistrate on a charge of having permitted 'a breach of the peace or riotous and disorderly conduct' within her premises in Jamaica Street. She was further charged with knowingly harbouring prostitutes on a regular basis. The charge was found proven and Mason was fined £5.

20 DECEMBER 1847 A crime described as 'a novel attempt at robbery' occurred on this date. A young woman who had formerly lodged with a family in Soho Street, had paid the family a visit in the evening. After visiting, she said goodnight to the family and left to go home. However, it appeared that the woman did not in fact leave the house, as thought by the family, but instead hid under a bed, where she remained until they had all gone to sleep. At this time, she emerged from her hiding place and proceeded to quietly make her way around the house stealing an assortment of articles of clothing, depositing them as she did so, on a table in the hallway to carry away. In all probability, she would have got away with these items, had she not gone back upstairs determined to steal a silver watch which she knew to be kept under the pillow of the owner of the house. In her attempt to take the watch, the astonished owner was awakened and immediately raised the alarm.

21 DECEMBER 1874 Margaret Harten appeared in court accused of having 'attacked and assaulted a female child to which she had given birth'. The charge detailed that Harten had covered the child in bed sheets in order to suffocate it. An alternative charge of 'concealment of pregnancy' was offered to Harten however, which she pleaded guilty to, and as a result was sentenced to twelve months' imprisonment. Due to the high child mortality rate and poverty at the time, it was

A newspaper clipping of the murder of Marion Gilchrist.

WHOLE CASE REVIEWED.

common for cases of infanticide such as this to be reduced to the lesser, 'concealment of pregnancy' charge.

22 DECEMBER **1908** In the west end of the city, the murder of Marion Gilchrist was reported. Described as 'an old and feeble lady', elderly Miss Gilchrist who lived alone, with the exception of a maid, was brutally murdered with robbery thought to be the motive. Miss Gilchrist's body had been discovered by the maid, who had returned from an errand and gone into the bedroom after seeing a man emerge from the room and run out of the house. There she found the old lady lying in front of the fire with her head and face covered in blood and bruises. On largely circumstantial evidence, a man named Oscar Slater was apprehended for the crime and convicted in May the following year, by a majority verdict. Slater had been identified by two witnesses as being the person they saw fleeing from the scene around the time of the murder, although nothing was found either at the scene or amongst Slater's belongings to link him with the crime, or indeed to Marion Gilchrist at all. He had, however, been seen prior to the night in question, hanging around in the vicinity of Miss Gilchrist's home, and soon after the murder he had left the country to go to America.

The death sentence was originally pronounced upon Slater, but a respite was later given whilst he was in Duke Street Prison awaiting his execution, and the sentence was reduced to penal servitude for life. Attention was again given to the case in 1914, due to there being sufficient doubts over Oscar Slater's guilt; however, no action was eventually taken. Many prominent personalities of the time became involved, convinced of Slater's innocence, with Sir Arthur Conan Doyle being one of those most active in campaigning to the Scottish Office. In 1927, Slater was released from Peterhead Prison after serving eighteen years, still maintaining his innocence.

Finally in 1928, the whole case was reviewed in the same court in which Slater had originally been tried, and it was decided that there was an element of misdirection by the court at the original trial. Oscar Slater had been at the time, pretending to be a dentist, whilst making a living from the proceeds of the prostitution of his partner. This knowledge it seems, had been enough to convince the jury of his bad character, and hence his guilt of the crime in question. Some weeks after the case review, Slater was awarded a payment of £6,000 in respect of the wrongful conviction.

23 DECEMBER **1851** At the Glasgow Circuit Court, Sally McVey was placed at the bar charged with murder, by putting several quantities of arsenic in coffee, tea, bread and milk, which she then gave to her husband, Thomas McVey. The couple lived in Greenock, and a surgeon from that area gave evidence that he had been passing by their house when Mrs McVey came out sobbing, telling him that her husband had been ill for a week and was now dying. The surgeon at the time had thought the man was dying from cholera, stating that as the symptoms of cholera and arsenic poisoning were quite similar, it had been difficult to distinguish between them. Another surgeon from the area, who had a drug shop in the Vennel, gave evidence that Mrs McVey had come into his shop to purchase arsenic on two occasions just prior to Thomas McVey's death, which she told him was to be used for killing rats. The surgeon, on hearing of the death, contacted the police with his suspicions. The jury, after hearing all the evidence, deliberated for half an hour before finding the charge against Mrs McVey not proven.

24 DECEMBER **1873** Mary McLean was tried on this date for the murder of her female child. McLean was charged with wrapping the baby, which was less that a week old, in a petticoat and a shawl, placing a stone inside the material and throwing the child into the Clyde, at the back of Govan Parish Church. The superintendent of the Govan Poorhouse gave evidence that McLean had been an inmate there during September and October and had given birth to a child whilst there. Another witness, who knew McLean, told the court that whilst McLean was away during September and October, she claimed she had been ill with cholera, but had denied having a child. Medical evidence given showed that the child could not have died from natural causes, but pointed towards death by suffocation rather than drowning. It was highlighted that this could have been caused by the child being wrapped in the blankets, or by an accident such as the mother holding the child too close to her whilst she was carrying it. As it was impossible to tell whether the child had been murdered or had been accidentally smothered, the jury returned a verdict of culpable homicide. Mary McLean was sentenced to five years' penal servitude.

25 DECEMBER **1846** A charge of murder was faced on this date by James Daly, accused of 'violently, wickedly and feloniously' attacking a weaver named David Lore in Bridgegate Street. Daly was said to have tripped Lore up, then had proceeded to strike him on the head, causing injuries from which Lore later died. A plea of insanity was tendered on Daly's behalf and evidence was given by Dr Hutcheson, physician to the Glasgow Lunatic Asylum, to the effect that Daly was 'labouring under that species of insanity technically called recurrent mania', making him prone to delusions. The court agreed that Daly was insane and therefore unfit to instruct his counsel or go to trial, and therefore ordered that he should be taken back to prison and detained there until an application was made for him to be removed to another facility.

26 DECEMBER **1850** At the Southern Police Court, Alexander Duff, described as 'an idle profligate and an old offender', was brought up on a charge of attempting to abstract money from the pocket of 'a decent countryman' named Alexander Hamilton, in a spirit shop in Eglinton Street. Duff's tactics were to approach strangers in the street and offer various services to them, usually treating them to a drink, then taking money from their pockets whilst they were distracted. On this occasion, however, Alexander Hamilton had caught Duff in the act and had handed him over to the police. Duff was sentenced to sixty days' imprisonment.

27 DECEMBER **1850** Owen Clancy, described as 'a smart youth' from Bridgegate Street, was convicted at the Southern Police Court of the theft of two pairs of Wellington boots, two pairs of ladies cloth boots and two pairs of laced leather boots from a cottage in Paterson Street, Kingston. Some time before, Clancy had carried out repairs to the business premises of the owner of the cottage, and claiming that he was destitute, had implored the man to give him employment of any kind. Out of compassion and sympathy for the boy, the man gave him work running errands from the house and assisting the servant. On the day in question, Clancy had been sent to an out house in the backyard to brush the boots, and when he had been gone for some time, the servant on looking for him, discovered he had gone and had taken the boots with him. Clancy was sentenced to sixty days' imprisonment.

28 DECEMBER **1898** John Playfair, described as 'a middle-aged man of respectable appearance' appeared in the High Court of Glasgow, charged with murdering Daniel McPherson. Playfair, who was said to have had 'malice and ill will' against McPherson, was accused of murdering him by beating him on the face and head with a poker. Playfair had been a lodger in the McPherson's home and on the day in question a quarrel had taken place, which had been heard by witnesses. When one of the other lodgers had returned home around half past six in the evening, she found McPherson lying dead in the kitchen with blood on his face. The jury, by a majority, found Playfair guilty of culpable homicide and he was sentenced to fifteen years' imprisonment.

29 DECEMBER **1847** A young man named MacIlraith, who was in a barber's shop in Bridgegate Street, had a dispute with one of the barber shop staff and, losing his temper, seized hold of a razor which was lying beside him and threatened the man with it. The young shop assistant who had been threatened then also grabbed a razor and a fight ensued, which ended in MacIlraith being slashed across the cheek from his cheek bone to his chin and bleeding profusely. The young shop assistant was taken into custody.

30 DECEMBER **1864** Mike McGlinchy was placed in the dock on this date, charged with the rape and assault of Margaret Addie, in Govan. McGlinchy was accused of seizing hold of Mrs Addie, punching her in the face, knocking her down, dragging her twenty yards along the ground into a field, kicking her and raping her whilst compressing her throat. He pleaded guilty to the charges, stating he was under the influence of alcohol at the time. Lord Ardmillan, on addressing McGlinchy reminded him that the crime of rape was a capital charge according to the law of Scotland, he could have been facing the death sentence. However, as the prosecution had not requested the death penalty, his Lordship on this occasion, was prepared to instead sentence him to imprisonment. Lord Ardmillan further stated, 'the law of this country protects the honour of a woman as much as the life of a human being, and there is no greater offence than the wilful and violent forcing of a woman.' McGlinchy was sentenced to penal servitude 'for the whole period of his actual life'.

31 DECEMBER   **1847**   An incident in a lodging house in Bridgegate, described as being of 'the lowest class', resulted in the death of Mary Davidson. At about five o'clock in the evening, Mrs Davidson and her husband James were, along with others, in the kitchen of a man named Kelly, the owner of the lodging house. A quarrel over some trivial matter seems to have taken place, which led to James Davidson kicking his wife's leg. This disturbance, however, soon passed over, and, an hour or two later, the couple proceeded, along with some of their fellow lodgers, to the house of a publican in the same street, where they all 'indulged freely in liquor'. A fresh quarrel then appears to have broken out between Davidson and his wife, due to Davidson being more familiar than his wife thought appropriate with another female, at which point Mrs Davidson threw a cup at her husband. This outbreak was also soon smoothed over, however, and a short time later the party left and returned to the lodging house, all considerably affected by the alcohol consumed. Mrs Davidson, a short time after retiring to bed, was heard calling for aid, and found by fellow lodgers to be vomiting blood profusely. Twenty minutes later she was dead, her death thought to have been caused by the bursting of a blood vessel. James Davidson was charged with murder after a witness stated that on returning home, a quarrel had broken out for the third time between the couple, with Davison being seen to kick his wife again.

BIBLIOGRAPHY

BOOKS

Douglas-Hamilton, James (ed.), *The Sheriff Court Districts* (Alteration of Boundaries) Order 1996, Office of Public Sector Information, 29 March, 1996

The Law Society of Scotland, *A General History of Scots Law* (Nineteenth Century)

Williamson, Elizabeth, Riches, Ann & Higgs, Malcolm, *The Buildings of Scotland: Glasgow*

Information has also been sourced online from the following organisations and websites:

Glasgow City Council

Glasgow Digital Library

Glasgow Humane Society

The Glasgow Police Museum

The National Archives of Scotland

NHS Greater Glasgow and Clyde

Scottish Court Service

The Scottish Government

Scottish Law Online

The University of Glasgow

University of Glasgow Archives

University of Glasgow Special Collections

Victorian Crime and Punishment

Wikipedia

www.sps.gov.uk

www.police-information.co.uk

www.archiveshub.ac.uk

www.glasgowhistory.co.uk

www.rls.org.uk

www.institutions.org.uk

www.mycityglasgow.co.uk

www.theglasgowstory.com

www.gorbalslive.org.uk

INDEX

Other titles published by The History Press

Paranormal Glasgow
GEOFF HOLDER

Paranormal Glasgow digs into the strange and peculiar stories of Scotland's greatest city. Here are tales of contemporary ghosts and historical hauntings, UFO and big-cat sightings, time slips, spontaneous human combustion, bizarre beliefs and urban legends. With more than 50 photographs, this collection by writer and paranormal specialist Geoff Holder will delight, unnerve and surprise visitors and residents alike.

978 0 7524 5420 7

Murder & Crime in Stirling
LYNNE WILSON

This absorbing collection delves into the villainous deeds that have taken place in Stirling during its long history. From cases as famous as the execution of Andrew Hardie and John Baird for high treason in 1820, to little-known crimes such as that of eighty-year-old Allan Mair, hung for the murder of his eighty-five-year old wife, Mary, in 1843, this book sheds a new light on the city's criminal history.

978 0 7524 6272 1

Haunted Stirling
DAVID KINNAIRD

This collection of stories contains both new and well-known spooky tales from around Stirling. A whole chapter is dedicated to the mysterious goings-on at Stirling Castle, where a 1930s photograph purports to capture the shadow of a phantom guardsman – possibly the same 'Highland Soldier' often reportedly mistaken by tourists for a castle guide.

978 0 7524 5844 1

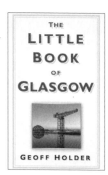

The Little Book of Glasgow
GEOFF HOLDER

The Little Book of Glasgow is a funny, fast-paced, fact-packed compendium of the sort of frivolous, fantastic or simply strange information which no-one will want to be without. A reference book and a quirky guide, this can be dipped in to time and a remarkably engaging little book, this is essential reading for visitors and locals alike.

978 0 7524 6004 8